Every Person's Life

Is Worth a Novel

Every Person's Life

Is Worth a Novel

Erving Polster

W · W · NORTON & COMPANY
New York
London

Library of Congress Cataloging-in-Publication Data

Polster, Erving.
Every person's life is worth a novel.

Includes index.
1. Psychotherapy–Case studies.   2. Psychotherapists.
3. Novelists.   4. Self-perception.   5. Human behavior.
I. Title.
RC480.5.P63   1987   616.89'14   86-31227

ISBN 0-393-30678-X

W.W. Norton & Company, Inc., 500 Fifth Avenue, New York, N.Y. 10110
W.W. Norton & Company Ltd., 37 Great Russell Street, London WC1B 3NU

1 2 3 4 5 6 7 8 9 0

To Miriam, Sarah, and Adam;

I like to say their names.

Contents

Preface

LUCKILY FOR ME, I started doing psychotherapy before I had completed my first graduate course in it. I was enthralled with everything I heard from my patients, as though I were five years old, lying on my belly listening to the grownups at family gatherings. I heard plenty from both groups of people, but to my newly assigned patients I had special responsibilities—with only the barest sense of what I might do. I knew that listening to their stories and replying naturally, as any responsive person might do, were not enough. That was the beginning of a 40-year quest to expand my technical savvy.

Now, with all that I have learned, technical and otherwise, I still recognize that my enthrallment with the people who come to me for therapy remains a major factor in my work. Nevertheless, within the reams of psychological writings I have read, there have been, with some notable exceptions, only tangential references to the fascinating nature of people's lives or how salutary it is for patients to feel this quality in themselves.

This book is an attempt to unite the technical requirements of a therapeutic job-to-be-done with the recognition of the healing effect which comes to people as they learn how remarkably interesting they are. No model for this union could serve my purposes better than that of the novelist, with whom the therapist has a kinship in the deep exploration of human behavior and awareness. By recognizing this common bond with the novelist, the therapist may more readily sense the drama in people's lives—the plots they live through, the suspense they create, the discovery of unique characteristics and events, the microcosmic commentary each person's life offers, and the inevitably creative passage through problematic experiences. This book will spell out a number of the ways in which the novelist's perspective may be transformed into therapeutic method.

The book's title—every person's life is worth a novel—is taken from a remark attributed to Gustave Flaubert, the great French novelist, who extracted drama from the lives of everyday people. In elaborating this theme, this book may also provide insights for many people who are not psychotherapists. Any person reading this book may be led to realize that he lives through experiences which, when rightly noticed, provide the stuff of which the most widely admired novels are composed. It is sometimes felt that novels are about characters from a world other than our own, although many of us do recognize ourselves in the characters designed by the novelist. Actually, we exist before the characters; the novelist and the therapist both invite us to open the covers of our own lives in order to find the marvels inside, painful or pleasurable. When we do, we move toward the *satisfactions of a confirmed existence.*

Acknowledgments

THERE ARE TIMES when writing a book feels a little like being shipwrecked with a typewriter on an unpopulated island. So, it was gratifying to discover there actually are people around to help out. I want to thank a number of those people whose help was important to me.

First, there is my daughter, Sarah Polster, a psychologist and writing consultant, with whom it was a special pleasure to talk about my writing. Her counsel and encouragement were a great support. She had also preceded me by having written a bachelor's thesis in 1975, entitled Scientific Method and the Glamour of Pain, in which she explored the relationship of psychology and literature.

I also received a big lift from Michael Miller, Herman Gadon, Natasha Josefowitz, and Tom Pace, who are friends and colleagues. They each read the manuscript in early draft and gave me sensitive and useful appraisals. My son, Adam, from a position outside of psychology, also helped.

I am especially grateful to my editors, Susan Barrows and Carol Houck Smith, whose discernment and thoroughness were invaluable.

I also want to thank Jane Olds for her warm-spirited typing of several drafts and Rina Szwarc, Ursula Freeman and Jayne Brown for the many generous secretarial contributions they made.

My strongest connections came with my wife, Miriam, who was lovingly available from start to finish. I was blessed to have her general support for the ideas in this book and also her many clear-minded opinions about specific passages.

Every Person's Life

Is Worth a Novel

ONE

Every Person's Life Is Worth a Novel

I am not talking about a script, Lydia. A script is a dialogue spoken in a particular setting. And a play moves singlemindedly towards a denouement. But a novel, the sort of novel one could imagine one's life to be, at any rate, seems to meander, with a ragbag of concerns.

—Lynne Sharon Schwartz
Disturbances in the Field

PEOPLE ARE often the last ones to recognize the drama in their own lives. They marvel at the adventures of others, but don't look inside to see that their own lives hold just as much possibility. Ralph was one of these people. If he had not been in my therapy group he would never have gotten my attention. He was a model of anonymity, indistinct as he sat there listening to other people's experiences. Silent all day long, though privately attentive to everything that was happening, he gave no hint that any of it held any relevance for him. Instead his face glowed emptily, like a turned-on light bulb.

Ralph's lonely luminosity was not crazy, although the constancy of it might make one wonder. He looked rather like an eastern guru — meditatively absorbed, expecting nothing from anybody else. He didn't look frightened, but it was obvious he wasn't going to say anything. I thought that talking might fracture the wholeness he was trying to hold together, a wholeness hung in midair, like the "OM" in a meditative chant. But how long could this protective wholeness last?

Smoked out by the pressure that had been quietly building up in him all day and finally realizing that the day might end without his having said a word, Ralph forced himself to speak. Right away I could see that my speculations had been wrong. Ralph's silence had not been part of a mystical formula; the unchanging facial tone was only one element in his typical disavowal of importance. From this one-down position, there remained an urgent wish to salvage something, but it was almost too late. As he finally tried to speak, he was apparently so numbed by silence that it had become altogether too easy for him to know nothing and say nothing. I tried to help him out of his paralysis but in response he could only mouth psychologese. Using all the familiar words to explain his immobilization, he said he was frightened by "challenge," by "making contact," by "change," and by "authority." That's as far as he could go in spelling out what he wanted to say. On the face of it, he was a jargonized shell.

However, I still had reason to believe that Ralph, under the right circumstances, would come across. Now that he had spoken, I intended to get past his blank mode and flesh out suggestions of interesting story line. There was already a wispy hint of sweet radiance, although he offered little incentive for any indifferent person to explore further. As a miner of experiences, I could recognize the signs of any number of other interesting characteristics, but I had to watch out for the contradictions with which he threw people off. He had intriguing green eyes, but they looked painted on and were shadowed by his protruding brow. The lines in his face turned downward, bespeaking an actively troubled depth, yet his look of resignation would distract most people from climbing down into those depths. His lithe body lines, intimating fluidity, were contradicted by his fixed posture. And in his empty expression one could envision a stonewalling toughness, like that of a caught spy. Already I had plenty to go on!

Yet, even if these contradictions had not been so evident, I would have been certain that the stuff of drama was there in Ralph; it is there in everybody. All people start with a journey through the uterine canal to enter a foreign world. Surviving the crisis of birth, people continue to live in life-threatening dependency upon unselected strangers, who speak an unknown language. They are intimidated by unpredictable events which make them cry, kick, scream, and bite. At other times, they are ecstatic. They undergo dramatic changes as they pass through various life phases, such as sucking, crawling, self-awareness, sexual swelling, and vocational discoveries — each of which provides new opportunities and new threats. Always, at whatever stage, they are bewildered by contradictions between their needs and the needs of others, who may have strange and often unassailable customs. Whether realizing it at the time or not, each person is recurrently party to mystery, violence, suspense, sex, ambition, and the uncertainty of personal resolutions. And eventually, there is death for all! Like a mountain stream that carves out a river bed, these and many other experiences cut through people's lives, engraving character.

No one can escape *being* interesting. People can *ignore* the profusion of influences, however, and many do so with exceptional talent. Ralph was unusually adept, like the cartoon character Mr. Magoo, who blindly walks through the most devastating dangers as though nothing is happening. Although Magoo is virtually blind, we, who are watching, can see his narrow escapes. We laugh hilariously as he comes through time and again without a scratch. Magoo delights us with the tempting delusion that we can get away with blithely ignoring the world around us. Many other imaginary characters are not so lucky as Magoo. Verdi's Camille dies of tuberculosis after ignoring her health and Tennessee Williams' Blanche DuBois lives in a dream world until she gets carted off to a madhouse.

Ralph's evasions were not as dramatic as Magoo's or Camille's or Blanche's. With those characters, the suspense about what might happen remains alive; we care right to the end. With Ralph that wasn't the case; the way he composed himself made it hard for others to care. So it is with many people. They may appear linguistically sterile, morally neuter, visually plain, or depleted in energy. However, these are all camouflage, intended to deflect from what is actually interesting. In my 40 years as a psychotherapist, I have seen great masters of camouflage. Some of them have been more skillful in hiding their exciting qualities than I in finding them. But I always know they are there, as the hunter always knows that the unseen snakes and birds and chameleons in the woods are there for the undeflected eye. Sooner or later, when I have alertly hung around, the faded person will usually come out of hiding. For moments, at least, he reveals something so arresting as to merit, like a character in a novel, even more widespread attention than the private reading of my special attention. In giving up the dulled image, such persons offer remarkably individualistic, suspenseful, and colorful memories, attitudes, expectations, and insights. Having revealed these hoarded gems, some will stay open and remain continuously interesting. Others will revert at the first sign of danger to the emptiness they have always banked on.

At first Ralph spoke only with a cliché-infected mind. He was all intention, nothing substantial. After playing for a while in his gobbledygook pen and finally realizing there would be no payoff, I got out. Instead of trying to satisfy his psychological ambitions, I lowered the stakes by looking only for those details which I knew he could give me and which nearly everyone would understand.

As a starter, I told him about a few events in my own life, hoping to establish credibility for the importance of one person's life to another. I told him I was born in Czechoslovakia and gave him some information about particular hardships my family and I experienced as foreigners in this country. Then, since turnabout is fair play, I could ask him where he was born without being dismissed as a simpleton. By this time he was willing, though stiff. At first he sounded like a card file: Born in Baltimore, Dad in the diplomatic corps, lived in Baltimore three years, another place two years, went to Catholic school for eight years, diagnosed cystic fibrosis. Cystic fibrosis! He was ready to slide right over this. When I stopped him, he elaborated matter of factly. "Spent my childhood, me and my two brothers, on a respirating machine three times a day." With these words his card-file style began to break down. Soon he started to cry, asking seriously, but with a shade of incredulity, "What seems so bad about it?" and adding, "You can stand it. It's no big deal." "No-big-deal" turned out to be the theme of his life. Nevertheless, his tears had already warmed him, and he then went on to describe—with the full attention to detail that a novelist would value—what his life had been like. Shots once a week, one in his ass and one in his arms. Sweat tests, wrapped under a 500-watt bulb for eight hours. Had to leave school every lunch hour to get on a respirator. Couldn't feel normal.

Then another stunner. The diagnosis of cystic fibrosis turned out to have been incorrect! "It's a terminal disease," Ralph said, "You die before you're 18." The misdiagnosis became apparent only because he hadn't died. Then he cried more deeply, still insisting through his tears that it was *no big deal.*

With the prospect of death facing them head-on all those years, most people would think it was a big deal. Even Ralph would, had he read it in a novel. When I asked him about the imminence of dying, he said, "It wasn't talked about that much. I guess I never really believed it. Kids don't believe that kind of stuff. We were members of a group, though, and everybody died. One of the kids I remember well had a bike. He died. This one other kid, he was black, he used to go with me all the time for the sweat tests and the shots, so we spent some time together. He died too. He was about 16 when he died. It's bad—it hurts."

By this time I was sitting close to Ralph and he just came into my arms and said, "It just fucking hurts—just hurts. When I think about my childhood I think about lots of things, but never that— ever." Now he let go even further and cried in my arms as if he were cracking open. When at last he opened his eyes he was amazed to see how rapt people were because he had long ago foreclosed on others being interested in him. With such a large stake in reducing his misery to "no big deal," Ralph had screened out the immense fact that while others were dying around him he continued to live. Worse than that, in screening out one thing he had also subtracted much more of his life. His crying now was like rain in a drought, releasing the agony contracted in his body, renewing his grief about the actual tragedy of those children who had died, and recognizing his own astonishing survival. Ralph, once realizing his singular existence, continued to value it. Two years later, after a number of important events, some joyous, some sad, he remarked warmly, "It's strange to be affected by my own life."

Everyday Drama

In drawing out the drama in Ralph's life, it was necessary to set aside prejudices about what is interesting. In therapy that is relatively easy, since the time is arranged especially for that purpose. Under ordinary circumstances, setting personal priorities aside in order to ferret out what is only obscurely interesting is less likely. People have such a large variety of purposes in mind that it is often much too distracting to probe for the hidden drama in the lives of others. To care about certain people and simply set others aside is a perfectly good bargain for most of us. If some people don't catch our interest, they just don't. We encounter this every day at parties, at work, in families, in politics, and even in walking the streets of a city. A life of unprejudiced attentiveness to everything is out of the question. Yet more modest expectations are within everybody's range; it is possible to appreciate the drama in one's own life and to lower the threshold for seeing it in others. To be open to these implicit dramas, even in small doses, can be pivotal in the enhancement of personal experience. As novelist Jerzy Kosinski has said, in a *Psychology Today* interview with Gail Sheehy,

> Nothing bars me from perceiving my life as a series of emotionally charged incidents, all strung out by memory... An incident is simply a moment of a life's drama of which we are aware as it takes place. This awareness and the intensity of it decides, in my view, whether our life is nothing but a barely perceived existence, or meaningful living. To intensify life, one must not only recognize each moment as an incident full of drama, but, above all, oneself as its chief protagonist.

Here is one woman Kosinski would recognize, a woman who had missed her chance to be the "chief protagonist" in her own life. In a therapy session with my wife, she complained that her father, in dying, had left her his shoes to fill. She described a death bed scene that ended with her father's head in her lap as he died. In the story, her father was the major character and she only a minor one. It was clear that she lived her life that way too.

The therapist asked her to tell her story again, this time making herself the main character. As she did this, this woman experienced herself as free of the legacy of walking in her father's shoes, free to be a person with a centrality of her own. The shift in her story was quite simple. She just described her own feelings as he died and found them to be as colorful and touching as anything she had previously said about *his* behavior. The accent on her centrality released her momentarily from the heavy weight of her dead father's shoes. Whether she was able to continue this freedom is unknown, but on this day at least her mind was opened to the possibilities of experiencing authorship of her own life.

People often squander their authorship. They don't grant the same importance to experiences in their own lives as they do to those of the characters in romantic novels or popular television soap operas. Instead, they set high standards for interesting experience, sifting life's waters with a large-holed fishing net, letting a lot go through untouched. They may think verbal fluency is necessary for others to be interested, or they may think they have to be affable, sexy, or famous. If they have ugly lip formation, quiet manner, ethnic dialect or naive political attitudes, they expect to be shunned. They will also turn their minds away from what they think they can't handle, avoiding what might infuriate them, entice them, confuse them, or frighten them. It is much easier to experience drama as consumers of novels, where events are often simplified, can be safely experienced, and have clear beginnings and endings. Only occasionally do readers use this drama as a stepping-stone, recognizing that the characters, with a few personalized changes, could be themselves, protagonists in their own lives rather than voyeurs of the fictional.

What often escapes notice are those simple events which give context and continuity to life. One person, for example, asked me what interesting things I was doing lately. Although I knew he wanted to know about bigger things, I told him how I had especially enjoyed walking across my house that morning to get a glass of water. The feel of my soft shoes against the wooden floor, the view outdoors as I passed my living room windows, the change of pace from my work, and the pleasures of just drinking water, one swallow after another—all of them mattered more at that moment than anything else I was up to. He smiled, bemused, thinking I just didn't feel like answering the question. Perhaps I should have told him how this experience of getting a glass of water joins with other experiences of daily life to provide the reality, the context, for more intense moments.

Alertness to everyday experience creates the background for special drama. If you can appreciate the timbre of a familiar voice, or sense the mystery of a helicopter swooping low over the house, or know the urgency of a sneeze in the middle of a sentence, or feel the anticipation in opening a certain letter, you will gain the linking experiences which give the wise, beautiful, adventuresome, far-reaching experiences the continuity within which they matter. A ride in an amusement park, a special gift, an evening with friends, an award in school, a defeat in a fight, a disappointment when stood up by a date—all help a person to claim the bits of existence which are the markers of a known life. There are a billion of these experiences, each of which, alone, is dismissible; in sequence they are the spark plugs for those climactic events to which people are more likely to pay homage. People who omit too many of these elemental experiences from their awareness may become frantically active, seeking other experience fruitful enough to make up for what has, usually unknowingly, been lost. Others do just the opposite, resigning themselves to a deadening accumulation of stale, zestless living. Hyperactivity, on the one hand, and deadening, on the other, are among the consequences of skipped-over experience.

Transforming the Ordinary into the Remarkable

Transforming the ordinary into the remarkable is one of life's recurrent and compelling themes. The extraordinary is just waiting in the background of the ordinary for an inspirational force to release it. Consider the Scarlet Pimpernel, the adventurous rescuer who masquerades as a foppish nobleman, the scullery maid who proves herself a princess by feeling a pea underneath many mattresses, the plain brown nightingale who sings more sweetly to the Chinese emperor than the bejeweled mechanical bird, saving his life, and Clark Kent, who turns into Superman. All are examples of the pervasive human wish to emerge from unexceptional guise as a unique and wonderful creature.

Contrasts need not be so marked for drama to be discernible. However, where the contrasts are smaller and where transformations from ordinary to remarkable are more easily attained, a fine sensitivity is required. An artist like Vermeer guides people to this sensitivity, looking not for the obviously special event, but instead for extraordinary grace in simple household moments. Bringing his eye to our own households, we may warmly mark the private familiarities of smoothing a bedcover, mending, fetching the newspaper, pouring a cup of coffee, taking warm clothes out of the dryer. Or, just outside, we may honor the sight of an elderly person crossing a busy street or a youngster mastering a bicycle. Such experiences give support and inspiration for the moment-to-moment focus, which offers a sense of continuity lacking in the more easily recognized highs and lows one may reach, for example, when falling in love or recovering from critical illness.

Novelists are foremost among artists delineating those experiences that many people omit from their personal awareness. In the opening lines of *Sister Carrie*, Theodore Dreiser tells of a moment of transition between a life at home and a life away—a moment of no return. He populates this moment with ordinary possessions, a surge of feeling, a taste of the past, and a hint of missed relationship. With his combination of simple awareness and fateful prospect he electrifies this moment. If not for Dreiser's skill in animating the simple experience, one could easily say Caroline Meeber just went off to Chicago for the first time. It is that and much more when he writes:

> When Caroline Meeber boarded the afternoon train for Chicago, her total outfit consisted of a small trunk, a cheap imitation alligator-skin satchel, a small lunch in a paper box, a scrap of paper with her sister's address in Van

Buren Street, and four dollars in money. It was in August 1889. She was 18 years of age, bright, timid and full of the illusions of ignorance and youth. Whatever touch of regret at parting characterized her thoughts, it was a farewell kiss, a touch in her throat when the cars clacked by the flour mill where her father worked by the day, a pathetic sigh as the familiar green environs of the village passed in review, and the threads which bound her so lightly to girlhood and home were irretrievably broken.

In this paragraph, everything that happens matters. Each detail contributes to the scene, our understanding, and the moment's suspense. Nothing is too small or too large to be included in the rush of words leading to the climactic sense of connections "irretrievably broken." By then, the details have lit up the implications of a great adventure begun.

For the psychotherapist, similarly intending to light up the experiences of a lifetime, everything that happens in a session has similar potential. Unlike in the novel, where each ingredient is already finely selected, in therapy many of the words, sensations, movements, and expectations will be superfluous. Yet, using the same creative selection process as the novelist, the therapist accentuates key experiences and provides leverage for the emerging dramas.

One woman, Jean, told me about calling home and remarked, incidentally, that her father answered the phone and "turned her over" to her mother. This incidental detail, elaborated, proved to be a spotlight, illuminating influential elements of her life. In everyday conversation one would slide past such phrases. The miniscule curve of her lip while saying it would be disregarded. A misty hopefulness would be passed over. As the tiny incident was elaborated, however, it became apparent that this woman felt lifelong disapproval by her father, who characteristically sloughed her off. Although in her generosity she always excused his rudeness as innocent ineptitude, she nevertheless felt the isolating effects of being unwelcome in his world, the world of adulthood. Her belief that something was wrong with *her* was altogether incongruous when, on the one hand, she saw her college professor father as though, alas, he were the family idiot, therefore unchangeable, while, on the other, she swallowed his judgment of her.

Actually, Jean was a remarkably beautiful person, one with whom most fathers would have felt blessed. Extrapolating from her words and my own disbelief that anyone would dismiss her, I guessed he loved her too much, not too little, and didn't know how to handle it. Would his feelings open him up to being captured? Would he be distanced from his career? Would he feel too awkward? Would loving make him feel like a sissy? Neither she nor he will probably ever know the answers to these questions. What she could do, though, with a slight boost in her confidence, was to help him to expand his recognition of her. She did this by gently encouraging him to stay on the phone with her a moment longer.

Once Jean realized that by feeling unworthy of a better relationship with her father she may have prematurely foreclosed changing it, she became free to be the guide rather than the outcast. She could actively bring him along to accept her rather than making foolish excuses for him. Soon she was able to extend their conversations and to change the quality of them. He was no stone, after all, and she became altogether less dismissible. She began to have unprecedented conversations with him, and later, without prodding, he visited her from his distant home. Once her mind opened to him, she also reached beyond him to find a new welcome in the world of adulthood. Her impact at work grew, and she fell in love with a man who, for the first time in her 30-year life, gave her the reciprocal love she had coming to her. When she married this man her father unfortunately reverted to his old ways by failing to come to the wedding. But then, his absence was more regrettable than debilitating.

INFLATION OF EXPERIENCE

As a paradigm for the therapist, showing the way toward recognizing valuable human experience, the novel comes closer to the scope of a person's actual life than do poems, plays, music, or sculpture. The time span and the variety of places encompassed by the novel provide a broader spectrum than is available in other art forms. When Flaubert said that every person's life is worth a novel, this was a testament to the large stock of happenings from which the novelist's work can be drawn.

From this stock novelists freely forage material; with shifts in emphasis, intensity and timing, their characters could be anybody. They put them through every form of dilemma, sometimes guiding and sometimes helplessly witnessing the way their characters carve out their lives. That they invite the inclusion of everything under the sun is well described by Henry James who, in paying homage to the writings of Honore de Balzac, says:

> . . . his subjects of illumination were the legends not merely of the saints, but of much more numerous uncanonized strugglers and sinners. . . . The figures he sees begin immediately to bristle with all their characteristics. Every mark and sign, outward and inward, that they possess; every virtue and every vice, every strength and every weakness, every passion and every habit, the sound of their voices, the expression of their eyes, the tricks of feature and limb, the buttons of their clothes, the food on their plates, the money in their pockets, the furniture in their houses, the secrets in their breasts, are all things that interest, that concern, that command him and that have, for the picture, significance, relation and value.

To apply an uncommonly lively receptivity to the "bristle" of living is a most fundamental task for the novelist and for the therapist. Yet there is a constant challenge to the person responding; sensitivity calls for a rightful choice from all that teeming presence. Milan Kundera, for example, in *The Unbearable Lightness of Being*, writes extensively of Tomas. He is a surgeon, but Kundera has chosen to give no description of his actual surgical work. On the other hand, Kundera makes sure that the relevance of Tomas' chance meeting with an old friend, not fully apparent at first, becomes apparent later. As large as the novelist's landscape is, it does contain a tight system of relevance; each detail matters in the total picture.

The same is true for therapy — perhaps even more so. Desultory conversation, for one thing, is regrettably rare. Much that a client might say while sitting around with friends never comes up. Partly because of time limitations, partly because of narrowed purpose, attention is given only to what seems immediately pertinent to getting better; what doesn't seem pertinent is commonly viewed as an evasive tactic and its acceptance as incompetent. Therefore, much that might be interesting, be it love of opera or a special hobby, may never arise. In attending to relevance, however necessary, both therapist and novelist face the danger of becoming so technically narrow that they present, paradoxically, only a caricature of any actual person.

This winnowing process is also inevitable, though less deliberate, in everyday life. We don't expect everything that happens to fit together. We do not even notice many of the people we pass on the street. What someone has said three days ago may be only a blur. These omissions are usually welcome, since they cut the huge glut of daily concerns down to a manageable few. Much of what happens is actually worth very little notice, a wisp of interest passing swiftly through consciousness. A stray impulse to quit a job, a flash of anger, even a suicidal thought — all minor in the lives of most people — may tilt a person's consciousness when given the inflated attention common to both therapy and fiction. An apt commentary on such inflationary hazards is given by Diane Johnson reviewing *Austin and Mabel* by Polly Longworth in the *New York Times* Book Review:

> Mabel Todd has all the attributes of the villainness in a novel of the period — a self-centered, trouble-making adulteress with a disdain for housework and altogether too much willingness to display any of her seemingly numberless and genuine talents — musical, dramatic, literary, artistic ... if she had been in a novel, Mabel would have to expect disgrace and painful death. As it was, she had only to endure a little gossip and disapproval, and that from by no means everybody, for she had her partisans.

Neurosis will also often inflate the importance of events or characteristics. A spanking does not really mark a person as evil, a failed test does not mean a person is stupid, and a smile from a date is no assurance of intimacy. "Life goes on" is a simple homily for setting proportions right. Although this saying may sometimes be rueful commentary, it also offers a peaceful option to overreacting. The novelist may sometimes want to show that life does go on and let a character go against society and get away with it. But the condensed world of the novel often calls for a lesson to be taught, a symbol to be created, an entertainment to be fashioned, a tragedy to be encompassed. Since so much is to be omitted, the mere writing down of that meager remainder of all that could be written guarantees that it will be given special significance by the writer, at least, and if successful, by the reader.

The therapist joins the novelist in making a big deal out of small selections from all that is actually happening, taking each event not only for its own sake but also for its meaning in an enlarged perspective. While participating in this artful inflation, we need to remember that things don't work that neatly in everyday life. Chance meetings with old friends, trips to the hardware store, lost car keys, and forgotten appointments may or may not slip right through the ordinary person's consciousness. But in the hands of the expert novelist or psychotherapist any of these events might be the focal point of a spellbinding story or a successful therapy. Everything counts; in daily living there is no such likelihood.

Since the importance of any experience is so subjective, everybody is faced with inflationary potential. Suppose, to illustrate the challenge, that a 45-year-old man has just had his all-time most exhilarating sexual experience with a 19-year-old woman. He starts a brand-new life. Now he wears tight jeans instead of a suit and tie. He is captivated by the newest musical fad and is no longer interested in his old friends. He leaves his wife, intending to live an unfettered life, and he gives up his job to work more independently as a freelance consultant. Judging from this bare-bones description, we might say that this man is inflating a temporarily delicious escapade. It is the kind of inflation common to manic people who go haywire; for them proportion is difficult to measure. If this man is indeed making more of this experience than it merits, he is soon going to be out in the cold.

It would be necessary for the novelist, if this man were his character, or the psychotherapist, if he were his patient, to wonder how this precipitous change would fit into a life which must take past and future into account. That's where good drama parts company with mere inflation. Some hint would be expected presaging the change—dreams of surprise and adventure, a sense of lifelong personal confinement from which the man is surging to be released, a supportable belief that he can pull this change off, a willingness to bet his life to rescue himself from the mundane. These hints may or may not be immediately observable. since a person's preparatory mental rearrangements are often subterranean. Given the variety of people's motivations, distinguishing inflation from drama requires a sensitive knowledge of the circumstances surrounding an experience.

Lacking either the sensitivity or opportunity to get the necessary insight, people will often follow custom in making their judgments. According to most standards, this 45-year-old reborn is inflating his sexual experience. Most people would agree that you just don't change your life that precipitously, setting aside all that has previously seemed dependable. The custom might very well be right in this man's case. If it is, he is in trouble. It also may be wrong, if his motivations genuinely call for great changes. An uncertain future with many fingers beckons to this man. By way of consolation, if he has made a reckless mistake, he might be able to benefit from his bumpy experience. The lessons learned become part of the "at least syndrome." *At least* he may learn endurance in the face of pain; *at least* he may experience the spiritedness of "going for it"; *at least* he may know the continuity of a self undergoing radical change; *at least* he may see how comical a turned-around head may be. Alas, the gloomy truth is that it would be better to have gotten it right the first time.

An example of someone who got it right over and over again is the father of writer Maureen Howard. In her description of her father's extravagant exits, she shows the fine line between that which is out of proportion and that which is endearingly unique. Her father always enlarged his minor departures from the house into major ones. He recognized, in his staging of the commonplace, that he was playing to an adoring audience. His farewells were always trumped up. At the same time, he implied a mystery about the world out there. He played on the suspense implicit in any farewell. He emphasized his importance to his children and theirs to him. He showed them his work as an actor, hinting at its shape. And he greatly pleased them. Here are Howard's words about her father:

An actor manque, my father had one routine that was magic and, though he never guessed it, was the very essence of the modern story-teller's art — worthy of Borges or Beckett. When he was going out someplace in particular, he'd stage his departure. Standing at the door in his coat and hat, he'd say: "I'm going away, but before I go I have something to say." And then with measured solemnity, with a hush of terror, with pride, pomposity, with tenderness — "I'm going away . . . " He put down his hat, unbuttoned his coat as if reconsidering but then, launched again with full resolve, hearty, upbeat, fearless, "I'm going away . . ."

Nothing followed. Neither plot nor meaning. It was all in the performance, what he invested in and yielded from a few silly words. I suppose it thrilled me absolutely, and left me strangely unfulfilled. In this version of why I've come to be a writer, I imagine that I want to hold an audience as completely as he held us at the kitchen table and at the same time, though it is hardly possible and cancels his game, have something to say.

The idiom of Howard's father, unforgettable to her, inflationary though it may have seemed, gained valid proportion because he always took his children into account, concocting his trickery as much for them as for himself. Not only were his amplified departures entertaining, but they also gave birth to an enthrallment in Howard which impelled her to continue, as a writer, what her father only hinted at as an actor.

Other themes more commonly satisfy the need for inflation. Sensational murder or divorce trials, love affairs of the famous, corruption in government, daring rescues, unbelievable wealth — all are amplifications ensuring popular attention. However, while corruption by powerful officials may be of concern to millions of people, it may provide no more drama for any one person than when he receives an extra $5 at the checkout counter. For the shopper, the moment of choice between honesty and dishonesty or between compassion for the clerk and the pleasure of getting away with some money is instant drama.

Personal experience has the power to surpass grander events. What *matters* to people is the essence of the divorce struggle of their friends, the grieving experience of relatives, the elation of a neighbor upon graduating from college after many frustrations. The arts, while risking inflation by lighting up the ordinary, open people's minds not only to the large effect but ultimately to their own perceptions, continuity, and context.

Rhythm Between Pain and Drama

The death of a son, dramatic when it occurs in a novel, is nothing less than traumatic in actual life. In the face of the pain, little attention is left for those other realities which may ultimately provide shape, meaning, proportion, or inspiration to the suffering person. For those who are in pain, the pain is all that counts. There is a figurative swelling which forms around it, ensuring that this presently unassimilable experience will receive all the attention it has coming. The swelling, by guaranteeing attention, is a barrier between *the* experience and all other experiencing. Those who try to restore perspective will only be rushing fruitlessly toward an unlikely rapprochement. Resolution depends on an evolving series of experiences, all serving to release the individual from confinement to the painful event.

It is only after the pain is lessened that the drama inherent in the tragedy may be honored. That is to say, once the painful event, whether current or remembered, is restored to membership in the whole of the person, the conditions for drama are formed. The event comes to accentuate a valid, though scarred, existence. This confirmation of existence, forged out of a severely narrowed consciousness, is the nucleus of drama. From this nucleus, one may expand beyond the nullifying prospect of pain, eclipsing it by seeing once again the actual range of what matters.

In the novel *Disturbances in the Field,* by Lynne Sharon Schwartz, Lydia has four magnificent children, whose sprightly minds and child-color freshen everything they touch. They are already intimates of the reader when the two youngest are killed in a bus crash. Lydia is enveloped in mourning. The shock is also great for the reader, who, through absorption with this family, has become a party to their devastation. Still, they are Lydia's children, not the reader's. Having this measure of distance—far enough away to prevent inconsolable pain and not so distant as to preclude a concentrated sadness—helps the reader to experience a larger scope for Lydia's life than she herself can muster. The reader knows, for example, that Lydia has two other great children, is blessed with musical talent, and has a marvelous husband, as well as unusually loving friends. Although all of this counts tangentially to Lydia, it doesn't measure up to dissolving the pain. Inside her pain there is little room for perspective. There wouldn't be for the readers either if the children had been theirs. But from their position they can see the hope for resolution. Nevertheless, while rooting for her, they are not sure Lydia will ever make it. It is possible that her pain will blind her permanently or until it is too late. For the reader, the suspense builds and builds. Meanwhile, for Lydia hope, suspense, and resolution are nonsense. Only the pain counts until she is able to catch up to the reader's perspective.

The word "drama," according to Webster, derives from the Greek "deed" or "act." For the person in pain, necessary deeds help to recover perspective and dissolve the pain. These deeds have great variety and include such commonplace behavior as crying, shivering, talking, telling stories, lamenting, going back to work, drinking hot toddy, going for long walks, or enjoying those people who are still there to be enjoyed. The psychotherapist is well aware that the individual is a charge-discharge organism and that staying up-to-date with oneself requires release of the energy which is stored up. The bottlenecks created by seemingly irreversible events or immutable self-images must be opened up. Sometimes the breakthrough is sudden, like the lancing of a boil. Usually, though, the release is more gradual, each single episode contributing to the total restoration. It is said that time heals all wounds, which means that in the natural course of actions a person's function keeps on registering, over and over, that that person is still intact and still has the basics of the pre-wound identity. The pain of mourning, of shame, and of failure is washed out as one's normal fluids course through the channels of self-awareness.

Whether restoration is quick or gradual, all solutions have in common some form of action that will discard a stuck perspective in favor of new possibilities in feeling and deed. As Derek Jacobi, the actor, has said, in an interview with Michiku Kakutani, acting is one opportunity to "ennoble all the sad, distressing things that happen to you in your life. . . . You can transform an emotion that was originally a hurtful one into something very soothing. For instance, my mother's death several years ago was hugely traumatic for me. And yet on stage . . . it is no longer hurtful inside. It's a kind of purging process." So, also, in therapy entry into the disturbing feelings of any person provides an opportunity to cast out those feelings instead of remaining with a stagnant self-image.

Narrative action served to flush the pain out of Daniel, a 30-year-old member of a therapy group. He was an affectionate, bright and engaging person, who was suffering over a frustrating love affair, one in which he felt awkward, inarticulate, selfish and disrespectful. In his misery he judged himself to be a creep and insisted he had always been a creep. Since pain obliterates contradiction, he could only give attention to things that would confirm his creepiness. Deciding to go along, I asked him to spell out his creepiness further. He then recalled how, in his adolescence, he had never known what to say to anyone. He gave us some unhappy anecdotes about those days, picking on himself mentally as he might have picked at adolescent pimples.

Among his stories was one about a high school dance, where he had naively humiliated a girl he had a crush on. The memory hit a special nerve and he began to cry. Crying was only further evidence of his creepiness. To the rest of us, listening from the outside, the story was a touching note in the wet, contorted comedy of adolescence, familiar to all of us. As Daniel continued to cry I pointed out that, although he judged his actions as creepy, he was actually just crying, spelled c-r-y-i-n-g. This wry reminder seemed to turn on a different switch and set him off on a new rush of adolescent stories that were in no way creepy. To his surprise, he remembered the time when he had shrewdly outwitted a bully who was out to get him for dating the bully's former girlfriend. Soon after telling this story Daniel began to laugh and went on with other recollections of his high school life — successes, funny and warm.

Daniel *had* survived adolescence, a notably torturous time. But he had so enveloped himself in his persona as creep that for years he had blocked the narrative of his life. Every chance he got, he reverted to his self-image as a creep, with critical judgments so rigid there was no way out. He was installed as a creep. When his labels of himself were replaced by action—telling stories and crying—new experiences appeared, as they always will. With the arrival of suspense, perspective and relief—important elements of drama—Daniel was then able to join with others in the group in personal celebration of his victory over youthful awkwardness. Soon after this, although drama would not require it, Daniel ended his frustrating love affair, without self-recrimination, and began a new, rich and more graceful relationship.

Had Daniel read, say, *Catcher in the Rye*, he would have easily recognized and sympathized with the struggles of an adolescent trying to catch up with those new complexities which make it hard for him to know what he feels and to say what he means. By means of drama, Salinger helped to clarify what would otherwise be only faintly known. Were Daniel to read *Catcher in the Rye* he would come to know that Holden Caulfield was no creep, even though some people in his life might think so.

The therapist, like the novelist, has cultivated a capacity for what Henry James calls the "prodigious entertainment of the vision," the zest to see what is there to be seen. What is obscured or disconnected is given a sense of direction and excitement, so that the patient feels he or she is going somewhere. Simple perceptions point the way. A stiffening upper lip, a look of muted horror, a contradiction between a tight jaw and a plea in the eyes will all serve as introductions to the dramatic life experiences. While looking and listening, one may also envision a bully, a swindler, a kid sister, a stubborn brat, a lothario, a traffic cop, a dancer, a lost love, a dethroned prince. With such casting of a person's life, the full artistry of the therapist, like the novelist, may honor the unrealized self by releasing all the poignancy, sadness, frustration, anguish, sweetness, love, fury—everything that belongs to the confirmation of a person's experience.

TWO

Living and Telling

Narrative is the art closest to the ordinary daily opera-
tion of the human mind. People find the meaning of
their lives in the idea of sequence, in conflict, in metaphor and in moral. People think and make judgments
from the confidence of narrative; anyone at any age is
able to tell the story of his or her life with authority.
Everyone all the time is in the act of composition, our
experience is an ongoing narrative within each of us.

—E. L. Doctorow,
"The Passion of Our Calling"

THE RAW MATERIAL for stories is always being formed. Each
moment in a person's life hosts an endless number of events.
Considering the abundance of this treasure, relatively few stories
emerge. Most events are given no more notice than the sound of
leaves rustling on a lawn or birdsong outside a window. Other
events, more influentially embedded, may receive unconscious notice—continued resentment, for example, of forgotten insults.
Clearly only a fraction of experience remains after the mind has
implacably excluded most of life's happenings from awareness.
Those events which live on in story form remained understandably dear and carry an enduring reality, linking together the select-

ed survivors of personal experience. Without this linkage, only the dimmest sense of reality would remain—isolated pulses, unmarked.

Jean Paul Sartre recognized the remarkable gift of meaningfulness and adventure that the story offers to all people. As Sartre giveth, however, he also taketh away through his gloomy view of the contradictions that sabotage a sense of enduring reality. Through his chief character in the novel *Nausea*, he says, "Nothing happens while you live. The scenery changes, people come in and out, that's all. . . . Days are tacked onto days without rhyme or reason, an interminable, monotonous addition." For Sartre's character, the answer to this nihilistic state is to tell about these happenings, and he even thinks, "for the most banal event to become an adventure, you must (and this is enough) begin to recount it." He goes on, though, to add his seemingly hopeless contradiction, "But you have to choose: live or tell." This means that if you only "live" there is nothing really there; the fleeting experience is nonsense, hardly worth the attention it commands. On the other hand, if you tell about it, it can, through the telling, be a vibrant, adventurous experience. But once you start doing that, the living is over. Then what is there to tell about!

Paradox is no stranger to human existence, however, and this one is neither more nor less vexing than others. Rather, by giving recognition to the paradox between raw living—untold—and confirmed living—that which is told—Sartre gives unaccustomed importance to storytelling, normally accorded a more lighthearted place. Although it is, of course, difficult to live something out and tell about it at the same time, this exclusiveness is softened by our remarkable integrative skills. This dexterity is evident everywhere, ranging from the crucial coordination of the disparate functions of our brain hemispheres to the frivolous trick of patting one's head while rubbing one's belly. This deftness is equally available for the coordination of living and telling, a feat which, in contradiction of Sartre's protagonist, we all accomplish everyday.

Of course, some people do it better than others. Some are fooled into mistaking the tales for the events themselves, repeating them over and over as though that will restore the old event itself. Some tell stories when they should have conversational exchanges.

Some distort the events that actually happened. Some tell stories that are marvelous elaborations on what was only a simple experience; for others the most complex event is worth only a grunt, the punctuation mark for a story to be imagined. Some people are wary about telling those things which they are afraid will make them look bad.

In spite of all this personal complexity, there remains a strong urge to tell. No one has described both the magnetism and the frustration of trying to connect the living and telling better than Jorge Luis Borges. He prized faithfulness of reproduction so highly that he wrote a haunting poem concerning it. In his poem, "The Other Tiger," he thinks of a tiger, one which actually lives in the jungle—his movements and the tracks he makes, his sniffing of deer, his stripes and quivering skin and his deadliness. In describing the tiger, "conjured," there is a weakening in the reality of the real tiger. He hopes to dream this reality into existence through his words but he knows the futility he faces. Nevertheless, an indomitable need compels him to seek out the third tiger, the one that comes to life in his dream. He says:

> Let us look for a third tiger. This one
> will be a form in my dream like all the others,
> a system and arrangement of human language,
> and not the tiger of the vertebrae
> which, out of reach of all mythology,
> paces the earth. I know all this, but something
> drives me to this ancient and vague adventure,
> unreasonable, and still I keep looking
> throughout the afternoon for the other tiger,
> the other tiger which is not in this poem.

Most storytellers would be satisfied with less than Borges, though all are trying to create reality over again, reconstructing what has already existed in another place at another time. Fortunately, for those of us not as talented as the great writers, intimate conversations do not require us to have their storytelling skills. The visibility of the teller's flesh, the previously established interest of the listener, the immediacy of response—all join to enrich the story.

Through intimacy, I may be as moved by my daughter's account of her experiences in Mexico as I would be by the finest novelist. Yet, everyone who reproduces reality must face Borges' challenge to more or less bring to new life what has actually already happened. One does not produce a carbon copy, but resuscitates some aspects of the original experience.

In many stories this revival is done poorly. People leave out secrets. They protect themselves from showing weakness, arrogance, foolishness, and all the other damning characteristics of an authentic report. Furthermore, contact between the teller and the listener may be of poor quality unless the telling takes account of timeliness, freshness, relevance, feelings, and credibility. If the stories bypass the present concerns of any of the participants—for instance, describing a recent quarrel when others are concerned about a friend's illness—annoyance, boredom, futility, vacancy, and similar troublesome effects will obviously result. If the storyteller relates trivial experiences that seem endless, there will be a large yawn. If the stories are only one-sided and do not allow for give-and-take, they may also slide away from the listener's mind. If the stories are obdurate and witless, repeatedly relating the same complaints, the listener may grimly wait for them to be over. Just because stories are natural does not give them privileged reception.

CONVERSATIONAL STORIES

Widespread as the varieties of storytelling are—including, at the least, such diverse forms as novels, history, music, political speechmaking, and sports broadcasting—the most active vehicle for storytelling is ordinary conversation. When someone asks as simple a question as what you have been doing lately, this is a request for a story. You are reciprocating with an elemental story when you say, "I just ran into Paul for the first time in years. He was in the supermarket and we're going to have lunch next Tuesday." This may be all the asker wants to know and all the teller wants to say. Most people, though, want to have more events in their stories. In this brief account there are already hints of an interesting story line. Paul sounds like a shadowy figure, distant yet possibly still relevant in the lives of the conversing people, who may be surprised about the supermarket meeting. The mystery of Paul's absence is joined with the mundane supermarket. There is some excitement about the arrangements to eat and talk together. Maybe an old intimacy will be recovered. What will be revealed? Paul may have been working in Wisconsin or just released from prison. If the listener knows Paul to be either bad news or the promise of new beginnings, the unfolding story will be more exciting than if the meeting is expected to be of little consequence.

High absorption or not, this is already a story—simply because an experience was recounted. People met, talked, renewed relationship, made arrangements, were recognized as party to the past and future. Telling about it gave increased dimension to the reality of the meeting, partly because talking adds a motor component to what otherwise would be only remembered, partly by providing witness to a meeting which might otherwise be passed over, and partly by creatively making a recent event live once more in spoken form. Furthermore, the storytelling experience produced a communal feeling by connecting the teller with the listener.

One well-known example of a conversation filled with stories is the movie "My Dinner with Andre." The telling of stories is central in this movie—that's all there is. Andre, a theater director, and Wally, an as yet unsuccessful playwright, are old friends getting together after years of lapsed relationship. Andre, who had disappeared, has now returned to New York, as though from the dead. At dinner he wants to tell Wally all about a number of his experiences, many of which have kept him on the borderline between satori and madness. Wally wants to hear these stories; at first he only listens, but later he tells some stories of his own.

Andre goes on at length, telling tales about the magical glow of Findhorn, so luminous that it blasted him into recurrent hallucinations; about elaborate communal happenings in fairy-like woods in Poland; and about other eerie events in such disparate places as Long Island and the Sahara. For most of the movie Wallie is enthralled with the strangeness and intelligence of this man, who extravagantly describes how he has discovered the magnificence of humankind.

As the conversation goes on, Wally begins to speak up for his own unadorned lifestyle. He has evidently discovered life's magnificence a lot more easily than Andre. In contrast with Andre's, Wally's experiences may seem hardly worth mentioning, but they are evocative of his own equally beloved style of living. He says, in response to Andre's exotic account, that he is just trying to survive, earn a living, and pay his rent and bills. He enjoys staying home with his wife, Debby, and reading Charlton Heston's autobiography. Now and then, he goes to a party or something and occasionally he gathers his little talent together and writes a play. And he enjoys reading about other little plays. He has a list of errands and responsibilities that he keeps in a notebook, and he enjoys going through a list carrying out the responsibilities and doing the errands and then crossing them off the list. This, and by implication much more that is comparable, is all that he needs in order to know that life is worthwhile. Andre's version is considerably more florid and drawn with more agile descriptive powers but no more serviceable in forming an enduring reality.

Different though their stories are, Andre and Wally share a common denominator in confirming previous experiences. The need to do this, over and over, reminds one of the myth of eternal return, as described by Milan Kundera in *The Unbearable Lightness of Being*. He says, not unlike Sartre, that only by recurrence does life take on substantiality. What is a war between two African kingdoms, he asks, if it alters "nothing in the destiny of the world even if a hundred thousand blacks perished in excruciating torment?" According to Kundera, transitory circumstance offers absolution to all experience. In further commentary, he says that anything that disappears is "like a shadow" and, no matter its horror or beauty, means nothing. He further quotes a German adage, "Einmal ist keinmal . . . what happens but once might as well not have happened at all. If we have only one life to live, we might as well not have lived at all."

The story serves as a prime vehicle for creating the recurrent experience Kundera envisions. It revives the mind's attention to prior experiences, presenting them anew, almost as though they were happening again. The better these reproductions, the more vividly the listener feels the new life a story may give to a previous event. Perhaps, as Borges suggests, the new life will be only a dim or distorted representation of the original, but through the telling there is at least a wisp of recognition, if not a wholehearted restoration. The teller and listener join in witness of recurrent existence, sadly short of immortality but knowing a life that is their very own.

LISTENING FOR STORIES

Stories must not only be told, but also heard. What is said gains value from the listener's understanding what has been said and his knowing that what has not yet been said may soon come to be said. Eudora Welty is one of the greats among listeners, listening not only *to* stories but *for* stories. She says, "Listening children know stories are *there*. When their elders sit and begin, children are just waiting and hoping for one to come out, like a mouse from its hole."

The listening psychotherapist is also on the prowl for the signs of a good story, though patients are often not open to having their stories sniffed out. One of my patients, a geologist who tended depressively to dismiss her life experiences, was speaking nondescriptly about Roger, a welder 10 years younger than she. He was courting her, but she wasn't romantically interested in him. In her judgment, he was pleasant and generous but not very compelling, even though she spent a lot of time with him. Because depressed feelings often come with failure to recognize the interesting, I wondered what she was overlooking in Roger just because she wasn't romantically involved. The contrast in their occupations was in itself noteworthy, he working as a sporadically employed welder and she a professional person. He was also in and out of town, had no stake in matters intellectual or cultural, and set unpressured simplicity as the keynote of his life — just the opposite of her introspective, cultured ways.

As we explored Roger's ways further, she told me he had been in her house alone one day while the phone next door rang incessantly. Irked, he finally went out and snipped the telephone wire. How strangely simple! Then she went on to tell about another time, when he was rammed by a car while waiting at a stop sign. When he got out to get the driver's name and other information, the man in the other car took off. Roger chased this man at 90 miles an hour until finally the fleeing man, a recent Mexican immigrant, scared half to death himself, stopped—but only after he had arrived in the part of town familiar to him. After arguing briefly, Roger got the needed information and left—a stupid chase for very little gain and he was lucky to get out of it unscathed. As my patient told these stories, this now unusual man came to life in my mind and hers, too. He might not be the other tiger that Borges divines but also not so pale as to be dismissed. She didn't have to live with him or to love him, but when she recognized the flavor of his existence she was able to give up some of her resigned flatness.

REINING IN THE ELUSIVENESS OF EXPERIENCE

Much of what happens in life floats on the periphery of awareness. Jane asks, for example, whether I thought Agnes was unfriendly to her; she has a hard time knowing. John seems to be talking more about his ex-wife recently, but I don't know why I think so. Agatha vaguely senses that there is more music in her life these days. These all represent dim awareness, suggestive but undependable. If we were to spell them out by telling stories, details would unfold, giving more information and greater clarity. Hints would become realizations, bare facts would expand like bread dough, feelings and their associations would be revealed. An example is the poet who is moved by seeing a tree, which is only the skeleton for what he wants to say. While telling about the tree, he may say that it beckons him to climb it or that he wants once again to pick its bark or that its branches form an umbrella. He may become clear about fertility or gnarledness or grace. When people see trees casually, they are only trees. For those who tell about them, they may be much more.

In psychotherapy, special attention is given to the elusiveness of experience. People want to change their lives but can't put their fingers on just what it would take. One such person was Ingrid, who in group therapy spoke about a general sense of shame, fear, and self-criticism, not tied to anything that would account for her feelings. She just thought she "should have it more together, be more confident, more successful, more loving and more accepting." Her concepts didn't stand strongly enough to hang a wish on them. When I pressed her to spell out what she was ashamed of, it took her a while to say that when she disagreed with people she got mad inside, gritted her teeth, and became silently unyielding. That, she said, was what she was ashamed of—the dishonesty of her silence. Suddenly her shame seemed a little less elusive, although it still required further embodiment. Then she added that her mother always preached honesty at all costs, even though when Ingrid practiced it, her mother couldn't handle it. When lying was immoral and truth was unpalatable, Ingrid, of course, found herself in a bind, so she wound up silent over the years and forgot why.

In an attempt to flesh out the story, I suggested that, rather than staying stuck with contradictions about truth, which only paralyzed her, she try an experiment in lying. I assured her it need be only for the moment. She got very excited, her worried looked changed to one that was loose, even a little wild. With tongue in cheek, she told the group about the really tough week she had, working so hard around the house that her fingers split open and her nails crumbled. She "cleaned at the office, watered plants, did lots and lots of work and lots and lots of reports, lots of letters."

At this point she was still caught in the phoniness of the lie. But she was getting warmer. There were giggles about all she had done for the people in her house when suddenly she realized she was thinking about some real truths she normally would not mention. Then she changed gears and went on to tell a true story about how she recently entertained Norwegian relatives. Plainly her experience by then was no longer elusive. She said proudly, "I cooked for these people, I entertained them, I listened to their problems, their frustrations, I poured them drinks, emptied their fucking ashtrays. I spoke Norwegian for them so they would like me and be entertained by me and I gave them all hugs and kisses and I cleaned the whole fucking house Norwegian style. I mean, I worked my fucking ass off. Then I set this beautiful table, with lace cloth and flowers and candles. I even asked my uncle to say a prayer before dinner, so they would feel at home and comfortable. Did this three nights in a row for three sets of people. I did an incredible job. . . . There is a lot of excitement to that."

At this point, she ruefully observed that in her family men were allowed to go on and on about their experiences, some very tall stories included, but the women were supposed to serve and tone themselves down. This realization clarified her sense of not being *counted*. By now, she *felt* counted and she couldn't care less about the roles she was supposed to play in her family. From then on, these feelings of shame simply evaporated.

By similar detailing and elaboration, stories in everyday life may also pin down the otherwise elusive experience. A friend called, for example, and I was on another line, long distance. I wanted to call her back when I was done but all she wanted was to know whether we could get together that night. I knew we couldn't but I didn't want to be peremptory. I didn't know why not; I knew her well enough not to stand on ceremony, but instead of just saying no I told her I would call her back in a moment. When I did, her line was busy! Several times the same thing. I concluded she was cool to me, but when I finally reached her she was quite warm. We talked a while and made arrangements for another time. Later, while telling my wife the story of what happened, I realized what I hadn't realized before. I was afraid that since I don't ordinarily talk much I would seem to be unfriendly. Actually, I am quite friendly and my friend accepts my quietness very well. Telling this story I knew this more clearly and was no longer bothered.

JOINING LIVES

We also use stories to join our lives with those of other people. One of the rewards of reading stories is that the reader becomes enmeshed with the characters, finding a new family of events to care about. In reading John Irving's novel, *The World According to Garp*, for example, I was so enmeshed with his characters that after a climactic automobile collision, in which one of Garp's young sons was killed, it took me a few days to get over my sadness. That was more than I had bargained for, but I accepted this involvement, distressing though it was. My sadness was a measure of my interest in the novel's characters. Many readers do not want that much involvement in fictional characters' lives. In fact, in a television interview, Irving once said, about an earlier novel, that he had received an irate letter from a reader who complained that she could no longer trust him because he put her into circumstances which she felt were wrong for her. He understood her point, although he felt that what he wrote was organically right, and he recognized his responsibility to readers—not to make their lives easy but also not trickily to bandy their emotions about.

This felt union is also a part of the psychotherapy relationship, which lies somewhere between fictional and real: fictional because of the highly stylized relationship, where the individuals are together only for a session and where the boundaries are therefore only a little more crossable than a book's boundaries; real because of the flesh and blood of the people. Furthermore, the identity of the creator of a story is more ambiguous in psychotherapy than in fiction. The story lines developed in therapy are jointly created; the therapist and patient are, one might almost say, co-authors. Sometimes the therapist is like the reader of a novel; it is, after all, not his life which receives direct focus and he listens avidly. In Eudora Welty's meaning, referred to earlier, he listens *for* stories and is highly sensitized to whether the unfolding story is a good one or ultimately won't fly. At other times, he not only listens but also guides the development of the story. He may set up experiments to encourage the patient's exploration both in the therapy room and outside of it. He may interpret, advise, or provoke. He may be supportive or informative. He works to get his patient headed in a direction that promises a better life.

Whatever the psychotherapist is doing, however, his freedom is limited. To be swept innocently into his patient's story is only half the requirement. The other is to maintain those critical faculties necessary for recognizing some of the qualities of good story line, as an editor might. Three of the qualities he looks for are coherence, directedness, and bearability, each of which will be a factor in effecting change.

First, in the service of *coherence*, the story, for dependable attention, must promise to hang together, each part eventually belonging to the whole. This coherence need not be unvarying; some incoherence will actually spice up the account, as long as the listener experiences mystery or intriguing implications. When the incoherence seems like mere chaos or when necessary consequences of any event are interminably delayed, attention will fade. Patchiness of experience exists in anybody's life, but for some these patches may feel well harmonized and for others they repre-

sent a torn personhood. The therapist is alerted to look for opportunities selectively to pull contradictions together so that they will
be experienced as valid members of the composite person. While
developing a confidence in basic coherence, one may go long stret-
ches without making clear sense; nevertheless, incoherence is often at the root of personal malaise. Everybody wants to be whole.

Secondly, therapist and patient will both need to sense a *direction* in which they are moving. Sometimes this is a clear direction,
as in getting a new job, smiling more easily, or bringing up previously taboo topics. Sometimes the movement, though nowhere
evident, may actually be going on and leap into awareness at a later
time. Neither reader nor novelist will countenance going nowhere
very long; nor should the therapist or patient put up with stagnan-
cy because of misguided personal tolerances. As John Gardner
says in *On Becoming a Novelist*: "The common reader demands
some reason to keep turning the pages. Two things can keep the
common reader going, argument or story. If an argument just
keeps saying the same thing, never progressing from a to b, or if a
story seems to be moving nowhere, the reader loses interest."

There are many therapy sessions that also go over the same
ground, each session a facsimile of the previous one. Until this is
corrected, even the most compelling theme will get stale, even
rotten. The most patient or rigid people need to experience movement and when they do, each movement will often breed a new
one. Since movement is, in a sense, inevitable, it is often only
necessary to notice its particular, sometimes overlooked, manifestations. Not uncommonly, success is already there, but it is as
difficult to recognize it as to create it. One person, for example,
said he wanted to be more warmly accepted by a certain group of
people. Though he enjoyed being with them and had considerable
influence, the relationship seemed distant. I pointed out that he
often thinks before talking and this might create distance between
him and others. He believed he *had* to think first. I showed him
that many of the things he said were already spoken without thinking. He was surprised to discover this was true and he just needed
to transfer what he unknowingly was already doing to the desired
situation. With practice he could increase his trust that talking
without thinking would be safe and natural. In fact, the results

showed up quickly in his next meeting with this group, when his fluency increased greatly and his warm feelings were reciprocated.

Third, as to *bearability*, it must be recognized that there is a level of pain or discomfort beyond which people are no longer able to function well. An acceptable proportion must be maintained — whether in a novel, therapy or everyday life — between pain and other aspects of living. Humor, irony, diversity of interests, a sense of adventure, mystery, love — all are story elements passed over by those people who are most imprisoned within their pain. Such persons can be only temporarily interesting, either in a novel or in life itself. Both novelist and therapist must take the heat off sufficiently, so that their readers and patients can remain fresh. For the therapist, this is especially difficult because some people come already steeped in such tortures as to becloud all else. Nevertheless, compassionate support, helpful information, glimmerings of new possibility, humorous observation, time to unfold, even medication will all increase the bearability of problems.

The following is an example of how coherence, directionality, and bearability may enter into a patient's unfolding story. A 35-year-old interior decorator, Carol, had been married for years to a man whom she liked but with whom she felt she couldn't stand to spend the rest of her life. She had temporarily separated from him, and had to decide whether to end her marriage or get back together. She wavered between the almost claustrophobic prospect of getting back together and the equally painful prospect of breaking up her family; her three children loved their father. She repeated this ambivalent theme over and over — wanting to get out of the marriage yet finding it unbearable to end it.

Dialogues between parts of herself, recounting of personal influences, insights, resolves, opening her mind to her husband's characteristics, and all other therapeutic vehicles notwithstanding, her story began to feel interminable. Neither coherence nor directionality nor bearability was on her side in her aborted story line. Without any of these qualities, she was on the brink of walling me off, as she already had walled off others in her life. I wanted to join with her again. She seemed to be using her therapy as a distraction from the requirement to make a choice. As long as she was in therapy, she could *believe* she was doing something rather than just being mired. Actually, the therapy was serving as an excuse for delay. But the pain was too great to make further delay acceptable. Thus, without deference to familiar psychological workthroughs and from my own careful judgment, I told her I thought she should go back to her husband. I spoke more like a Dutch uncle than a psychologist, joining her as much as I could. Of course, she didn't like my advice, but she wouldn't have liked any. However, the necessities of good story line called for her to get moving.

She spent the next week furious with me. Her fury led her, however, to coherence, directionality and bearability. She had two new realizations, each of which added *coherence*. First, she believed my advice implied that she was a helpless child who needed to be returned to a supportive atmosphere. She felt insulted, although she was also aware that she was the one casting herself in the helpless child role. Second, she recognized a mountainous stubbornness in herself, one which required her to remain free of her husband. While recognizing this stubbornness, she realized she was trying to show up her mother, whom she had silently scorned for living all her life married to a man she did not love. As she expressed these new thoughts, her behaviors came together in my mind as well as hers, making sense to both of us.

At the same time, she also got across a new sense of the *bearability* of her experiences. She told me, in no uncertain terms, that she was actually very good at taking care of the children's food, clothes, health, and schooling, that she also took care of banking chores and accounts, made enough money to have a surplus, was doing the best professional work of her life, took out the garbage, loved her kids dependably, advised them and laughed with them. Her eloquence erased the agony by which she would otherwise have been routinely preoccupied.

Further, her sense of *directionality* was enhanced because she had gotten together with her husband, in spite of opposing my advice, to set up some ground rules for renewing their relationship — no pressure from him, for example, for either sex or permanent recommitment. This didn't work, however, and she ended their relationship again. Some time later, perhaps a year, when she then wanted to reunite with him, it was too late. By then he no longer wanted her. Although this was accompanied by some new pain, it was, in another respect, a freeing experience. Her life at that point had taken a new "spiritual" direction and she said she was living peacefully, free of both depression and a sense of being victimized by life.

In one respect, this story has a tragic ending because when she finally wanted her husband he was no longer available. Yet, tragedy is partly a matter of where a story ends.

LEARNING LESSONS

Stories often guide people in how to live their lives. Sometimes this purpose, clearly intentional, is served by moral or instructional messages. At other times the messages are not so obvious, only incidentally derived from the stories. Among the best-known carriers of messages are the stories of the Bible, sufi stories, literary stories — those of Charles Dickens, for example, the fairy tales and myths from which children learn much about the morality of our culture, and the stories of pop culture, found in songs, contemporary books, movies, and television.

Through the story of the manna which fell from heaven, we confirm the munificence of God and the power of following Him. Through the story of Christ and Mary Magdalene, we discover that sinners are redeemable. One sufi story tells about a community warned that if they didn't hoard the existing water they would wind up drinking a new water that would drive them mad. Only one man hoarded the old water. He was able to drink his own water while others were left to drink the new. He saw they were indeed mad but they, in the security of their community of new ways, thought he was the mad one. Finally, desperately lonely, he decided to drink the new water. Soon he behaved like all the rest. He abandoned, even forgot about, his own water and became accepted again in the community of people, who welcomed the miracle of his return to sanity. The effect of the general lesson, that madness is a relative matter and that one of its alternatives is to knuckle down to community norms, is strengthened by the story.

Fairy tales also highlight the circumstances we all have to endure. Hansel and Gretel remind us of the evil forces in life and of the vulnerability of children to these forces. Happily they show us that virtue and innocence are superior to venality; we may all feel encouraged that it is possible to win out even against great odds.

As for the current pop culture and its teaching effects, there is considerable controversy. Some say violence has increased because the TV and movies are accenting violence. Others say the stories do no such thing; they only give people the entertainment they want or harmlessly release pent-up violence. Without entering into the pros and cons of this controversy, we can say that certain stories on TV will get across points more vividly than nonstoried instruction. Not too long ago there was a program about an incestuous relationship between father and daughter. The story, explicitly didactic, clearly intended to affect society's attitudes about incest. After the program, viewers and people caught in incest binds kept the telephones busy in agencies dealing with these issues.

In psychotherapy a story may be told to reveal principles of living and to flesh them out with action details. One example is an account by Dr. Lynda Gaynor, a colleague who attended a case seminar taught by my wife, Dr. Miriam Polster, and me. Dr. Gaynor told us about a patient who characteristically maintained a distanced stance in his life, both generally and in his relationship with Dr. Gaynor. Nevertheless, in spite of this debilitating gap in his contacts with people, he managed, quite surprisingly, to retain his girlfriend's romantic interest in him, his friends' social interest in him, and Dr. Gaynor's interest in him as her patient. But he was not happy.

Recognizing her patient's ability to keep people interested while he himself maintained distance, Dr. Gaynor was reminded of a visit to an art museum in Avignon, where in the courtyard a number of peacocks and peahens were cavorting. It was mating season, and Dr. Gaynor told him what she had observed. She said, "I was fascinated to watch the peacocks approach a female, spreading and raising their magnificent tails, displaying their brilliant plumage, and fanning the air until it hissed with agitation. The female would ignore them, however, continuing to peck at the ground. The peacock, undaunted, would change his angle of approach, repeating his display of colors, but without the slightest show of interest from the female. Finally, after numerous tries from many angles, he would drop his head, close up his fan of a tail, and slowly drag himself away. He would get about 15 feet away. Then the hen would look up from her activity, turn her head toward the peacock and make a tiny "Peep"—at which the peacock would come running back, tail spread—and begin the entire procedure again." Dr. Gaynor's patient, though shrugging as usual at the time of the story, reminded her of it months later, but his greater involvement in both therapy and other relationships started right away.

INFORMATION

Since many stories are creations of the imagination, it may seem contradictory to think of them as sources of information or as historical accounts. Yet they are. Many novels reveal prodigious knowledge. When the protagonist is an architect, the novelist must learn enough about architecture to give authenticity to the characterization. For a novel to be set in Egypt, the novelist must know Egypt—perhaps its history, perhaps the habits of its people, perhaps its geography, perhaps its government, its food preparation, the character of the desert, etc. Henry James wrote about this informational gift when he said about Balzac:

> Balzac's France was both inspiring enough for an immense prose epic and reducible enough for a report or a chart ... it was as a patient historian, a Benedectine of the actual, the living painter of his time, that he regarded himself and handled his material. All painters of manners and fashions, if we will, are historians, even when they least don the uniform: Fielding, Dickens, Thackeray, George Eliot, Hawthorne. . . . (Balzac) with an imagination of the highest power, an unequalled intensity of vision ... saw his subject in the light of science as well, in the light of the bearing of all its parts on each other, and under pressure of a passion for exactitude, an appetite, the appetite of an ogre, for *all* the kinds of facts. . . . Of imagination on one side all compact, he was on the other an

insatiable reporter of the immediate, the material, the current combination, and perpetually moved by the historian's impulse to fix, preserve and explain them.

Similarly, a major portion of the information of therapy is derived from the stories that people tell. One of the most innovative contributions of psychoanalysis was to establish a new form of information-gathering—not from case history interviews, as was customary, but from the evocation of extensive storytelling. The question-and-answer method of gathering facts had commonly resulted in only a narrow range of information, a lot of facts about birthplace, siblings and vocation. It was far too narrow for knowing a person well. In psychoanalysis, dry information-giving was replaced by free association, each patient unfolding the many chapters of his life experiences. Free association, though not requiring stories, invariably resulted in a flood of them. With the evocative guidance of the analyst, people were led to perhaps the most searching efforts in history into the details of their own lives.

As with Borges' other tiger, the original reality was not faithfully reproduced by these stories, but the new reality had its own vibrant existence. Because of this discrepancy, some would say that the original facts were not even very important, that what we *imagine* to have happened is what determines our perspectives and our behavior. Yet it is, after all, only the original event which spawns the new story. If it disappears, there is no "other tiger" to create.

A recent controversy in psychoanalytic circles, created by Jeffrey Masson, centers around this concern. He says that Freud's postulation of the oedipus complex resulted from his abandonment of an earlier belief that his patients had been *actually* seduced in childhood. Freud came to believe that these people had only *imagined* the seductions. Since there was no actual sexual contact, he inferred that there must be a basic human reflex to imagine the triangular sexual conflict among mother, father and child. This theoretical inference elevated the importance of imagination and subtly diminished the importance of information. If it didn't matter whether people were *actually* seduced as children, what information would matter? Whether a consequence of this point of view or not, psychotherapists have often been more interested in how people *feel* about their lives than about the facts of their lives. There is the joke about a patient who, when asked whether therapy had changed anything in his life, replied, "No, it hasn't but now I feel better about it." Although it is true that this lesson has benefitted many people by teaching them how to grow beyond the debilitating facts of their lives, simply dismissing these facts leaves a flimsy basis for one's experience. Whether one has been actually seduced sexually is a point of information that differs from imagination, much as Borges' real tiger differs from his other tiger. What may be at stake in differentiating between the two tigers is whether one gets eaten up or not. To be played with sexually at four years of age will have a continuing flesh and blood reality; if that is ignored, one could never feel taken seriously. Information is the takeoff point for the perceiving mind, as well as its confirmation.

A patient of mine pointed up this need for uniting information and extrapolation when he told me one day about a party he had attended. In his sessions he was generally very subdued in manner, but at this party he had played a guitar. This was a bit of information which surprised me because I imagined him to be a very private and withdrawn person who would not have allowed himself to face an audience. I asked if he would bring his guitar in and play some songs for me. When he did, his singing was a revelation—robust, melodic, loose. His fear of becoming a wild man, which had caused his subdued manner, apparently disappeared while singing. When I asked him to speak with the same energy available to his singing self, he could see that his victory over wildness while singing could carry over to ordinary conversation. How could I, his therapist, have known this man without knowing he sang to the tune of his own guitar?

DISCHARGE OF ENERGY

Storytelling also helps us to get rid of stuck energy when direct action is not possible. Sometimes this is easily done. If you have seen an automobile accident on a highway, the image of it may linger in your mind with no immediate outlet. Nothing more may be needed than to tell about it. Other calls to discharge energy may be more complex: a forgotten obligation returned to mind, an itinerary to be developed, a person to invite for the bowling team, and a conversation prematurely ended. All of these require something to be done; telling about them bridges the time lapse before something can be done. Telling about these unfinished tasks may also help clarify what one wants to do about them, creating a more enlightened, confident, and graceful personal readiness to do what needs to be done.

In psychotherapy this simple need to release undischarged energy has had far-reaching recognition, forming the foundation for some methodologies. Gestalt therapy, for one, theorizes that people live with a surge to complete unfinished business and that getting up-to-date requires a discharge of this interrupted energy. If a person is phobic about getting into elevators, he needs opportunities to discharge the energy that he is afraid would be released. Telling about the days when his parents locked him in a closet will give him such an opportunity. While he tells this story of being locked in a closet, large feelings may grow. These may be accompanied by powerful words, amplified breathing, screaming, imagining new ways of talking to his parents, forgiving his parents, new recognitions of current security, and any of the innumerable vehicles available, as we shall see, for creating new movement in interrupted old stories.

The story has more malleability than the originally frozen events. Since one is no longer bound by the old perceptual limits, one can see unexpected possibilities. Within the new borders, however, the patient may still be chary. The therapist, more experienced, provides the support, inspiration and editorial acumen, while the patient provides his material and dares to find out where the story line may lead this time around.

THREE

Transition–A Key for Stories

> ... at the very instant of concentration, the unchanging given is dissolving into many possibilities and is seen to be a potentiality.
>
> Perls, Hefferline, and Goodman, 1951

IN CREATING STORIES, authors, therapists, and everyday storytellers are all guided by the compelling presence of the *transitional* experience. Standing against an illusory sense of arrested time, so apparent in the stuck points of a person's life, is the knowledge that to live well one must recognize the inexorability of time's passage. One thing inevitably follows another, and if a person's attention moves gracefully from one thing to the next, there is a measure of excitement inherent to this process. The excitement happens so readily that it is only occasionally noted. One recognizable sign is the thrill of traveling at high speeds whether on a bicycle going downhill or in an auto going 90 miles an hour. Speed thrusts people into nextness, accenting the transition point, as it changes palpably in each instant.

For the reader to get an immediate crack at a simple transitional experience, I suggest this experiment. As you continue to read, alter your focus slightly by not only attending to the present word but also simultaneously anticipating the next one. Nextness is the key angle. You are always in between and always moving. Notice whether it makes a difference in your reading experience when you consciously lean into nextness. You will probably have tapped into a reservoir of your energy, creating alertness, excitement and fluidity. Leaning forward might also have cost you a measure of comprehension, particularly if you have moved ahead more quickly than you can readily coordinate. If you have already been accustomed to focusing on the transitional, it is probably easier; many people already do this spontaneously, actively anticipating nextness.

There may be some eyebrows raised by this perspective. Isn't this a frantic way to live, always alert to whatever is next, never settling into whatever is already going on, rushing headlong into the future? Although we may, of course, stumble over ourselves trying to get ahead into nextness or trying to predict what is next, what is proposed here is nothing so clamorous as that. Rather, it is a reminder of the naturalness of movement into the future—normally effortless and unconscious. A telephone rings and we head toward it. A sentence emerges from a string of individual words. A question is followed by an answer. Events flow naturally, one after the other, just like the more elemental sequences of inhaling and exhaling or landing after leaping.

THE ARROW PHENOMENON

This trip through continuity is, of course, not always as easy as these reflexive and peaceful sequences might intimate. Instead, the management of sequences is often filled with complexities and dangers that slow people down or even stop them in their tracks. Every event, whether as simple as a single word or a flickering in facial color or as complex as a policy announcement by the government, will point *arrows* into the future. As one illustration, consider the headwaiter in a restaurant who says, "Your table is ready now." Almost always, if you hear these words you will readily follow the waiter to your table. The arrow and the direction are clear. Even in this simple exchange, however, there may be elements which create greater complexity. You might have wanted a table outdoors and the waiter is leading you indoors, you might have waited an hour and feel either relieved or annoyed, or you might suddenly remember a phone call you must make. Nevertheless, in spite of various possibilities, the arrow will most likely move you toward the table.

Where there is a larger array of competing arrows, greater sensitivity will be required. Suppose, for example, that a woman friend says to me, "I want to call Henry." Simple words, leading to a simple act. If, however, I foresee unhappy implications when she calls Henry, I might warn her against it. Or I might remain silent, believing I shouldn't interfere and hoping it will not work out as badly as I suspect it might. The arrows may imply other directions as well. I may be relieved as I think that at last she is going to call Henry. Or, knowing my friend as I do, I may realize that she doesn't really want to call Henry herself, that she would prefer that I do it. Then I may offer to make the call. Or I may tell her to get on with it and do it. What I choose is important because if I choose insensitively from among diverse signs, there will be interruptions in the grace of our movement as my friend goes her way and I go mine. Sometimes this will provoke severe incompatibility. More commonly there will be only a vague sense of not getting anywhere. Unfortunately, just such missed connections will often decay relationships.

Here is an example of a few short exchanges with a research biologist, who was a patient of mine. I had been encouraging him to talk more than he does about his activities — to the woman he lives with and to others. In response, he said, "It's a lot easier to talk about things I am excited about and that are going real well than about things that make me really frustrated." There were a number of arrows here that I could follow. I wondered about his need for things to be *easy*. A whole story could evolve around that single theme. I passed that one up. Then there was the word *talk*. Did he prefer showing people things to telling them? Who listened when he talked and who pulled down the shutters? I didn't follow that arrow either. Then there was the word *excited*. What excited him and what happened to him when he got excited? That didn't draw me either. Any of these might have been prime arrows for other people or for me at another time. This time, though, the arrow I followed was his difficulty telling about things that *frustrated* him. I wanted to know more about his keeping frustration out of his repertoire. So I said to him, "Frustration is interesting too. Novels and movies are filled with frustrating events."

So, he told me about his work which was, according to him, "99% frustrating." I asked him to spell out what was so frustrating. After some generalizations he went on to tell me about one of his experiments. In spite of knowing little about biology, I became engrossed in his description of working with two proteins that are very similar but serve quite different metabolic roles. He gave details of his time-pressured struggle to crack the problem and told how, after about a week of work, he "finally got very lucky and found a way to solve it." He told the story of his frustrating research well and while telling it presented any number of new arrows in pointing toward new nextnesses. His allusion to luck was the one I rode.

Embedded in his reference to luck were two contradictory possibilities. One was that he was blessed with nature's bountifulness, a lovely feeling to have but not one that he ever exhibited. The other was that he was belittling himself, ignoring his own strong role in finding the solution. So I said, "*Lucky* sounds like you had nothing to do with it. I'd like to know more about your luck." As he went on, he soon recognized that he had made a skillful guess in experimenting with proportions of the proteins and how they would affect each other. In further acceptance of his own role, he recognized that good research allows luck its best chance to work. That made him a partner of luck, rather than a passive recipient.

In summary, during these simple sequences this man told a story with important elements of drama. The characters were chemicals, not people, but he gave a lively account of how these characters related to each other and what happened to them in one or another set of circumstances. He allowed his frustration to be a part of his story, facing up to it and feeling the fun in it. He described the risk of making certain choices and, as it happened, created a happy ending, although that would not be required. Furthermore, as a vehicle for personal message, the story gave him a good perspective on luck and a precedent for accepting his own competence.

There are many experiences where the connections are not so apparent and where the interval between arrow and consequence is much longer. One unmarried woman came to see me because she was pregnant and in a quandary about whether to have the baby. She urgently wanted the baby, yet she was not confident she could handle it all by herself. The prospective father loved her and wanted to marry her. Even knowing she did not want to marry him, he was willing to share responsibilities for raising the child, while making no claims on her. The woman was understandably afraid that these arrangements, even with all good intentions, would inevitably tie her into more of a relationship with him than she wanted—and she just *knew* they would not be good for each other.

The simultaneous arrows—to have the baby or not to have the baby—were so contradictory that I suggested she carry on a dialogue in which she role played her two options. While speaking for each side in alternating exchanges, her voice became resonant, her words became clear and resolute, she began to feel exhilarated instead of subdued, and she began to recognize her strengths instead of her inadequacies. On that note the session ended.

I expected that her recognition of inner strength would lead her to ahead and have the baby alone. But, as it turned out, I read the arrows wrongly. A week later she told me that the very exhilaration and confidence that had reappeared in the dialogue had led her to realize she did not need a baby. She felt peaceful about giving it up. She then had an abortion, altogether clear in her decision and in her newfound freedom. A further surprise came later. A man she had loved 15 years earlier on an Egyptian archaelogical dig reappeared. That relationship is now flourishing and they are soon to marry. This time a baby may come with whole-hearted assent.

SUSPENSE

Uncertainty is at the root of the dramatic experience. When attention is focused on what will be happening next, it gives a lift to each experience; it creates suspense. As E. M. Forster says in *The Writer's Craft*:

> We are like Scheherazade's husband in that we want to know what happens next . . . That is universal and that is why the backbone of a novel has to be a story. Some of us want to know nothing else—there is nothing in us but primeval curiosity. . . . (The story) is a narrative of events arranged in their time sequence—dinner coming after breakfast, Tuesday after Monday, decay after death, and so on. *Qua* story, it can have only one merit: that of making the audience want to know what happens next. And conversely it can have only one fault: that of making the audience not want to know what happens next.

Because they can telescope time, novelists enjoy a great advantage over therapists in this tilt toward nextness. Readers don't have to wait long for important consequences. In a few hours they will know whether people are going to get married, whether revenge will be successfully taken, or whether a change in jobs will work out. This shortening of interval magnifies the awareness of nextness. In ordinary circumstances it is easy for us to pass over the small transitions from one moment to another. We are free instead, since nextness is a state of mind, to look ahead to whatever we *care* about next. This option creates some long intervals between now and next, as well as suspense that may be harder to bear than comparable suspense in a book. In real life it might take two years to find out who the murderer is—or we might never find out. Plainly, a level of tension and suspense which would be bearable for the time required to read a novel cannot be sustained throughout psychotherapy.

In therapy, suspense appears unbearable, it is often met with resignation. The patient assumes a fixed position, foreclosing future possibilities. If the suspense can be reduced to a manageable level, a belief in these future possibilities may be restored. It would, in fact, be a great relief to the patient to see once again the readily attainable requirements of the future.

With this in mind, I asked Byron, a therapy group member who looked excruciatingly distressed, whether it was OK with him to be as silent during group sessions as he had been. I wondered whether he would consider even this mild inquiry intrusive; however, he was actually relieved and gave a simple explanation of his silence. He said he was impressed that the other people could talk about things that mattered so much to them. He himself would be ashamed to talk about those things that mattered as much to him. I suggested that by listening to others he might be getting ready to do so in the near future. He agreed. When I asked him how this future prospect felt to him, his demeanor changed. He smiled shyly, saying he was glad and that, more importantly, he no longer felt isolated. Apparently, having both a present reality and an announced future made him feel like a valid member of the group and gave meaning to his stuckness — even though he wasn't doing what they were doing. The fact that he *might* talk changed his experience from resignation to suspense. His silence became a precursor. Although we weren't placing any large demands on him, we were now all looking forward to the day when he would say what he wanted to say.

Manageable suspense keeps life interesting. People spoil if they have no suspense in their lives or if suspense lasts too long. We all know people who can subtly infuse expectation. They may do it with surprising turns of phrase. Or they may have mobile faces which move easily from grin to glower. Or they may tell compelling stories, or use hand movements which sweep us forward, or create a sense of urgency with their ideas. Whatever they say or do makes us interested in what is coming next.

One of these naturals at creating suspense was Ilana, a 40-year-old woman in a therapy group. She was not aware of anything special about herself, though everyone else was. She had large eyes, which immediately drew attention and promised animated words. When she spoke, her words came rapidly and with a Woody Allen type of self-deprecation. Her serious statements were punctuated by warm bursts of humor. At these points, her mouth would suddenly open wide, showing bright white teeth. Then the smile would disappear, leaving an odd look of imprisonment, her eyes flitting and her head tilted as though trying to see around the corner, worried but indomitable.

She conveyed a feeling that *everything* was important, but in a posture that implied she was only visiting for the moment. She joked around, looking as though the junior high school principal was about to call her in for having unauthorized fun. But she always escaped the authorities, saying things that were clever, wise, or funny. The other group members were transfixed when she spoke, awaiting each word. An internal cheer went up in her listeners every time she finished speaking.

How well this charm might work for other people depends on whether they would allow the suspense to move in fruitful directions. Ilana's suspenseful intimations, potentially nothing more than those of an endearing junior high school curiosity, led into stories of a woman who knew what she was talking about, adding substance to her charm. Her young mannerisms would soon prove empty if she had no subject matter or if her stories didn't go anywhere. Getting somewhere is what makes suspense a worthwhile aspect of lively attention.

ENDINGS

The concern with what will happen next turns ultimately into a concern with how things will end. Because the trip toward endings is often a rough one, burdened with delay, diversion and defeat, people become distractingly mindful about how things will end, neglecting the intervening events between now and then. To partially satisfy their preoccupation with endings they go to fortune tellers, skip over to the last pages of a book, daydream, or scare themselves with catastrophic expectations.

The famous slogan, "all's well that ends well," holds true for many experiences. The terror of being swept out by a riptide is gone after one is rescued. The anxiety when 16-year-olds are three hours late disappears when they arrive home. The threat of a dangerous illness vanishes when the x-ray shows a clean picture. Clearly, people usually accommodate well when their troubles end well.

This is not always so, of course, because some people, once frightened, chronically foresee bad endings. Others counteract this by compulsively making everything look better than it actually is. Hollywood, particularly in its early years, was especially well-known for happy endings, even when the novels from which the movies were adapted ended tragically. But, of course, Hollywood didn't invent the happy ending. Here is a simple-minded ending to an obscure novel of the 1880s. It represents a genre which exaggerates the importance of endings:

> And Margaret, still beautiful, with hair as white as snow, and a face as fair and pink as a pale rose-leaf, sat smiling and listening, and knitting beside him; no fears in any of their hearts to beat away, no strife to heal, the past unsighed for, the future sure, they made a picture of old age, well won,
>   "Serene and bright
> And lovely as the Shetland night."

Such an ending is obviously dated — remarkably square nowadays and perhaps laughable even in its own day. By contrast, reality has made its presence grimly known in the present century, particularly so since our worldwide wars and the advent of existentialism. The wars and existentialists both starkly remind people of the permanently obvious — that none of us is going to get out of this world alive. Worse, not only must we all die but there is also likely to be considerable anguish along the way. These bleak realities are nothing new. Throughout the ages, the alarm bells have been rung in Greek tragedies, the Old Testament, the New Testament, Shakespearean tragedies and modern tragedies. Yet, even though tragedy is old hat, it is also our very own. In our era there is a fresh recognition of the fates which trample over us, spinning and cutting the thread of human existence according to their own shrouded logic. Personal violence, wars, governmental suppression, fraud and slander are brought into homes daily through TV, newspaper, and friends' anecdotes. One person, living unexceptionally in New York, said he didn't know anyone who hadn't had a close relative or friend either mugged, robbed, or raped. These dangers breed an infectious wariness, keeping people alert to troubles in life and hyper-responsive to reports about them. In recognition of such an atmosphere, the arts — sometimes prophetic, sometimes reactive — have conveyed people through agonizing circumstances, often making it seem as if the tragic view and wisdom were inseparable.

Not only are there absorbing tragedies in life, but it is also widely believed that *life is tragic*. As John Fowles' writer-hero in *Daniel Martin* says:

> It had become offensive, in an intellectually privileged class, to suggest publicly that anything might turn out well in this world. Even when things . . . did in private actually turn out well one dared not say so artistically . . . only a tragic, absurdist, black comic view . . . of human destiny could be counted truly representative and serious.

This dark, cynical, prejudicial ethos, within which excellence is measured by facing up to death and its debilitative cousins, can exercise a ruthless debunking not only of happy experience but of most experience — even where neither happiness nor tragedy is of immediate concern. Within this tragic ethos, even so serious a writer as Eugene O'Neill has been skewered. Robert Berkvist, in a *New York Times* article, points out that O'Neill was attacked for writing a happy ending to *Anna Christie*; he was accused of seeking public satisfaction and approval. Feeling enraged and misunderstood, O'Neill replied:

> I wanted to have the audience leave with a deep feeling of life flowing on, of the past which is never the past — but always the birth of the future — of a problem solved for the moment but by the very nature of its solution involving new problems.

O'Neill's remarks emphasize the continuity which happy endings nourish. In a sense, what is happy about a happy ending is that it says things will go on. Tragedy is the opposite. It ruptures continuity. The tragic event *seems* to bring the curtain down inexorably. That is perhaps tragedy's definitive condition. When a person experiences permanent disfigurement, incontrovertible shame, or the death of a loved one, it may seem that everything she identifies with is ended. One might say that the person in tragedy is no longer the person she was and no other identity is acceptable. If, for example, a person has lost a leg, that is actually the end of *that* person, the one with two legs. As long as *that* person is the only one who matters, continuity is over. If she, less drastically, had lost a tooth, her identity would probably be disturbed but not annihilated. Each person has her own identity requirements; when these are severely breached, only a willingness to experience a new identity will restore continuity.

In the movie "Inside Moves," a young man is seriously crippled after trying to kill himself by leaping off a building. He is, at last, trying to live with his new identity as a cripple and is making a first timid move to join a group of disabled veterans who are playing poker. They know all about the identity problems which follow grave physical insult. One veteran is blind, another is in a wheelchair, yet another has two prostheses instead of hands. One of them asks the young man how he came to be crippled. He haltingly replies that he tried to kill himself. There is a pause while this sinks in and then one of the veterans says, "You've got it backwards; first you get crippled, *then* you try to kill yourself."

These folks have all discovered that their identities are not as fixed as they had believed during their most tragic period. The unthinkable loss has gradually become familiar, a testament to human versatility. Many people cannot achieve such transformation. When the only wish they recognize is unachievable, like the restoration of a beloved dead son, they will remain frozen in place. When in time they come to appreciate a simple conversation, a bite of food, a wry memory, a felt cry, or a recognition of friendship, they are on the way to replacing their loss. When, however, as may sadly happen, the discovery of continuing options is missing, all that is left is a lingering life, one where a single-minded identity has ended.

One such person caught in the grip of tragedy came to me for therapy because of a miserable relationship with her husband, a violinist. She had had an enjoyable affair with him while he was married to another woman. Some months after the wife found out about the affair, she had a heart attack and died. This was a stunning blow, especially as my patient was convinced the affair had precipitated the heart attack. Then she married the man anyway. After the marriage, however, there was practically no sex; subsequently, alienation set in. She was even stressed by his musician friends who visited and played music that would have given lovely color to most houses but only grated on her nerves. A taciturn man, anyway, her husband didn't know what hit him. All he could do was go mute and hold his ground.

From the beginning of therapy, it seemed evident that the previous wife's death had ended my patient's sense of herself as a moral person. Although the connection between her affair and the woman's heart attack was murky, because of previous heart disorder, she nevertheless continued to feel guilty and to blame her husband as well. The guilt kept gaining strength because, paradoxically, her moral standing depended on her belief that she had been irretrievably immoral. Instead of focusing on her continuing life, where she had many pleasurable opportunities, she became absorbed with strict judgments of her husband's behavior and attitudes.

There were two chief therapeutic tasks. One was to turn her raw pain into interesting conversation. This was a delicate matter because I aroused her wrath when my standards about childrearing, sex, work, schooling or any other themes were less rigid than hers. She would interpret my differences as opposition to *her* views, which I actually believed to have much merit—and we would have lively, eloquent conversations about these differences, which always turned out to be less drastic than she supposed.

The second task was to lead her into discovering how human it is to err. At first the errors were all mine. However, each time she came to accept me even though my "flaws" caused her anguish. Through accepting me, she also incidentally became less harsh on herself. We went through ups and downs but, as she experienced the human limits of her quest for morality, she became more nearly able to transform her *shame*—which punitively narrows her—into *humility*, which offers better proportions in self-acceptance. Humility permits both flaw and forgiveness and is an excellent antidote to shame. By now, she has become more open to laughing, has gained needed weight, has a new glow on her face, has started to have sex again with her husband, is going back to painting and has arranged for future work. Her character had seemed fractured by tragedy, but her life actually kept on moving. She had only to join the movement.

Novelists deal with the tragic prospect less prejudicially than do psychotherapists. They are free to let the chips fall where they may and can furnish the lives of their characters with experiences which neither they nor their readers would willingly allow in their own lives. The therapist, on the other hand, is commissioned to generate happy endings. This is made difficult by the complicated fact that while the therapist must try to save his patient from tragedy, he must also know the tragic factors in life and face them unflinchingly.

Novels help readers to know the tragic realities by expanding and clarifying the mind's dimensions, as the reader safely witnesses many varieties of experience not otherwise permitted. While reading a novel such as Flaubert's *Madame Bovary*, while absorbing her experience, the reader can navigate through her world with greater wisdom than was available to her. Readers may wish to call out to her and to offer good advice. In actual life, we do not know so clearly what to call out to our friends. Madame Bovary was much more obviously consorting unwisely with a doomed future than most people do. Real lives move more slowly, allowing many more turns and retractions and giving less opportunity for the bird's-eye view. Even when the reader is as clear in real life as he is about Madame Bovary, plainly one person's clarity will fall on another's deaf ears. Still, futile or not, many people are drawn to calling out in order to affect real-life endings.

Unfortunately, rescuing people has gotten a bad name in modern psychotherapy, partly because it is easy to fail but also because it implies robbing a person of independence and her own true destiny. Many people neither want it nor need it. However, in a world where people are naturally interdependent rescuing is a noble act. Human survival is predicated on mutuality, and it is a cold measurement that leaves a needy person to her own deficient resources "for her own good."

THE UNIT OF EXPERIENCE

Although the ominous prospect of a tragic ending gives dramatic impact to all experiences, endings are only rarely tragic. Nor are they usually happy. What is more pervasive than any measure of tragedy or happiness is that endings, along with beginnings, form the boundaries for the units of experience of which any life is composed. The existence of these units, approximate though they are, will heighten the sense of continual transition as it contributes to the freshness of living. Without the framing function that endings share with beginnings, life's shape would be indiscernible, each event melting into an unimaginable oneness. A word could not exist, nor *a* meal, nor *a* day. With such a vital charge, the recognition, even anticipation, of beginnings and endings is no minor phenomenon. It is the means for setting things apart and for uniting them. Together the reverberating exchanges between sequences of experience, each related to others, fashion a sparkling life. This interweaving of now and next is familiar in the individual firings of an auto engine or individual frames of movie films, each unit creating continuous motion by linking with the next. In these and other linkages, where endings and beginnings are gracefully joined, they often become undistinguishable from one another. As it is said biblically, in my end is my beginning.

These units are very personalized. Some people, entering their place of work, will say hello and feel that exchange is completed. Others do not feel finished until they have chatted for a while. Still others have a specific thought that must be expressed. Most of the time, though, people don't require finely-honed perception of units of experience. When a person decides she has had enough to eat, the meal, for her, is ended. It is more difficult to discern the end of larger units of life such as a visit, a marriage, or a job. Only rarely does anyone care to make a point of exact endings. Instead, people find great overlapping areas, which do not fall into orderly sequences. Something always occurs within something else. First there is the grand arc of a person's total lifetime. Then, within the individual's lifespan there are certain large units, such as childhood, a particular friendship, or the time lived in St. Louis. Further, people experience extremely small units, such as a shrug, a stray thought or a skipped heartbeat. There are also those units in between—a conversation with a friend, a walk in the park, watering the plants, etc. Through all these experiences, people learn to appreciate both the merging of events and the inevitability of endings. Death is the supreme ending and its spector is the most galling source of anxiety and carefulness. However, the greater the acceptance of endless endings, the more people are able to reverse an old saying and realize that "A hero dies a thousand deaths; a coward dies but once."

Even the most miserable lives include many happy units. Ghetto Jews, in spite of pogroms and poverty, had many happy family celebrations. Students pressed against the wall by examinations and failure will take time out for a beer. A parent losing two children at birth will love the third. To ignore the anguish in these circumstances would be the height of pollyanish deflection. To allow them exclusive attention, however, disregarding other discrete units of living, would be to surrender salvageable experience to the tragic image. The ideal in personal growth is harmony between very important priorities, like surviving in a terrorized neighborhood, and the many ongoing, unsymbolic, even paltry experiences. A full breath here, a live smile there, a vigorous moment, a vibrant color—all reverberate within the margins of the potentially overriding larger purposes. The psychotherapist and the novelist both place their bets on the recovery of these small elements as the substructure supporting the suspenseful prospect for good endings.

LINEARITY

The emphasis on transitional experience must take into account the eccentricities with which experiences often occur. Often, events do not follow one another in any simple cause and effect way. They do not have recognizable relevance to one another. Further, people do not always agree on the correctness of any particular sequence. The mind is an unruly instrument, hospitable to juxtapositions of events, often manifestly chaotic. As the chaotic unfolds, the originally obscure directions which these events are taking may well be recognized. That is the faith which many people practice—that there is an underlying intelligence which they bring to all events that will ultimately bend these events toward a recognizable whole. It is extravagant to say that all will actually be revealed in time; however, it is useful to give the organizational reflexes of the mind the necessary time to make sense and use out of what originally may seem senseless and useless. If we are flexible in connecting sequences, much that is given time to unfold will develop fruitful direction. There are three manifestations of this flexibility: skipping steps, sidetracking, and tightening or loosening of sequentiality.

Skipping Steps

When people want something badly they will often try to get it by skipping those steps that are normally taken. This may be very simple, like wanting dessert first. It may also involve becoming a carpenter without spending time as an apprentice or going into fifth grade without fourth. When people skip steps, they are allowing their own individualized pace to determine their sequences. Actually, these people may not be skipping steps at all if their own pace has readied them for a step for which others would not be ready. Each person has the option of dealing with her own sense of what is next, sometimes guided by the common steps and sometimes altogether free of this guidance. Though commonality offers many benefits — security, the wisdom of the collective experience, harmony with the pacing of other people — it also threatens individuality.

The individualized mind is naturally filled with peculiar connections, often showing no signs of the source of these connections or what follows. Sometimes these loose connections seem crazy. At other times, this looseness gives behavior a personalized stamp, cutting through the red tape created by ordained nextness. An applicant for a job, being interviewed by the boss, may start off strangely by telling him they would be better off meeting first on the golf course. A patient may tell her therapist to write her an outline for the projected therapy. An eight-year-old may walk into her uncle's house and, before even saying hello or assessing whether her uncle is listening, tell him she made the best drawing in class. In Kafka's *The Castle*, K leaves for the inn early in the morning, travels a couple of hours and when he arrives it is getting dark. In *Alice in Wonderland*, all is topsy-turvy. Such peculiar timing may often cause a double take and may also be stupidly abrasive, but fruitful function often depends on a leaping mind.

Here is an experience with a 30-year-old patient in a therapy group where leaps beyond the obvious next step evoked information and feelings unlikely to evolve from carefully arranged sequences. Carl was a cocky man, disparaging everybody—people in the group as well as other important people in his life. When he talked, his focus was on me, the leader; nobody else counted. When group members became angry about this, he was taken aback. But he realized he was deferent to some people and had very little use for most others.

In those days, I smoked a cigar, and at one point Carl suddenly asked for a match so that he could light it. Taking cues from his deference to me, I skipped a few steps and, instead of accepting his light, asked if he would like to sit on my knee. He hedged, but my leap had caught him off guard. Though confused about sitting on my knee, he suddenly looked very open and warm about my invitation. Before he could do it, I skipped again by asking whether he had ever sat on his father's knee. He had indeed. Then the story poured out. In summary, he used to take showers with his father until he was 14, felt very close to him, and was able to kiss him in public anytime he wanted to. Then, alas, when he was 15, his father died. This loss overwhelmed him and he suffered for years. As he told this story, his voice became soft. Then I asked him to talk to his father, which he did warmly and without either sadness or guilt. Visibly at peace, he turned to the rest of the people in the room and, no longer wary, for the first time talked to them as equals.

Another person, a 30-year-old woman, was trying to skip too many steps. The therapeutic task was to bring her back to a manageable step-by-step process. Carol said she wanted to be a great therapist—not a good one, but a great one. That is a lot to ask for. Without many intervening steps, she might as well try to swallow an elephant. In looking for a more accessible next step, together we recognized that her need for privacy moderated her impact on people. Carol's privacy subtly contradicted her therapeutic purpose. She conveyed a nonverbal message that self-revelation was "low-class." As long as her patients received that message, no matter how much she overtly encouraged self-revelation, a fraction of her inspirational force would be lost—just enough to disrupt the prospects for full expression. A more immediate step than that of greatness would be for Carol, a warm and potentially colorful person, to take the shades off her existence. Rather than trying to skip so many steps between her current level of competence and greatness, she now could take an intermediate step — turning her private life outward.

She took this step by telling the group that she was the daughter of holocaust parents. The origins of her privacy soon became apparent. Even though her parents told her some hellish stories privately, they believed complaining about their suffering to others was beneath them. Now, instead of adhering to the family's prideful reticence, she told us a poignant story of their uncountable daily indignities, including the shaving of her mother's head. Her sincerity, simplicity, and sadness in telling her story were moving in themselves. But her effect went much further. Others in the group, having been influenced by her, told their stories. By transcending her privacy she had opened up the atmosphere in the group itself.

How far along the road to greatness this experience will take her belongs in another chapter of her life. In her quest this experience has taught her to make her ambitions bite size and to let each success point the way. Also, whether she gets there is not all that counts. She may, at some point, not even be interested in greatness. She may come to prefer peace, the company of simple people, a place in the country, or a workmanlike career. Although the need for greatness guides her now, in her life she will have many guides.

Sidetracking

Sidetracking, the second form of sequence flexibility, goes off on a tangent from whatever is already happening. Suppose I am searching for an Indian belt to give my wife. I can't find the one I want, but I delay leaving the store when I discover the salesperson is a cousin of a man I knew long ago. We talk a while about him. While we are talking, long after I would normally have left, a customer comes in to return an Indian belt. It is a great belt and I take it. Such simple serendipities are familiar, but they are less likely to happen to people who have tunnel vision, plunging grimly forward, unsidetrackable. When openings are left for the unexpected to happen, the chances that they will indeed happen are increased.

Unfortunately, in therapy this harvest of the free mind is limited because patients, and often therapists too, are likely to be resolutely anchored to their purpose. This narrow vision creates a dilemma. On the one hand, the therapist must respect the patient's given interests, fixed though they may be. On the other hand, it is also necessary to provide fresh perspective to what seems inexorably stale. Both purposes may be served when the sidetrack taken is only a detour, leading back eventually to the original goal. Sometimes these sidetracks are surrealistically strange and only obscurely related to the original theme, but often they follow quite naturally from the subject matter of therapy.

Alma, a member of a therapy group, was asked why she seemed sad. She said she was still sad about her abortion six months ago and went on to tell about it again, fruitlessly, monotonously, and weightily, as though this were the core of her life. Actually, she had a lot more going on, as I well knew. Her sadness was important and could not be dismissed, but this was a conversation already cooked, like an overdone stew.

A detour made all the difference. I sidetracked her by asking her about her work. Her relatively new job was exactly right for her, giving her for the first time in a few years the gift of being marvelously appreciated. Originally only half-time and temporary, her job had now been turned into a full-time permanent job, with full insurance, as well as other, benefits. After she talked animatedly about her work for some time, we returned to the subject of her abortion. This time, however, warmed up as she was, she spoke vigorously. She turned angry toward the man who would have been the father, as well as toward her self-centered mother. When she was done voicing her anger, she began talking about finding a man with whom, this time, she *would* be willing to have a baby. Her sadness was no longer linked with resignation; instead it was a starting point for replacing what she had lost.

While this sidetracking experience was not very far out, others diverge greatly from the open highway. Imagine, for example, that a flavorless and boyish-looking man is telling me how his mother once more disappointed him. I have the option of directly examining that disappointment or fancifully sidetracking. Suppose, taking the second option, that I close my eyes and tell him I see a motherless calf sucking on a dripping water faucet. I want to call out to the calf that he needs milk but I am afraid he won't understand me and so I give up. Then suppose I go on to tell my patient how I grew up on a farm. I milked cows, hoed earth, worked 14 hours a day, ate huge meals, and had to have one of my fingers amputated. When I was 16, I felt like I was in a vise and ran away. I tell him I thought about the farm again just the other day, wondering whether anybody is still working it or whether it has been sold to land developers. Then, when we get back to his mother disappointing him, he is off the beaten track and can speak about his mother in a different voice, having gotten the freedom messages embedded in my story.

For those who are on friendly terms with their surrealistic stream of attention, the wandering mind will feel not so much like a gap in time as like a leap into a mysterious sequence. These so-called nonlinear juxtapositions do not actually bypass linearity. What they bypass is a common criterion of linearity—transparent relevance of each remark to whatever may be the recognizable subject matter. In the surrealistic mode, thoughts may follow one another in a seemingly gratuitous manner, torn out of understandable sequentiality. Yet, such sidetracking, when sensitively done, is all part of one fabric, each thought cryptically continuing what the other has begun. Sidetracking from a given theme and returning refreshed is a testament to the secret relatedness of disparate aspects of life.

Tight and Loose Sequentiality

The third opportunity for flexibility is to tighten or loosen sequentiality. Where sequences are tight, the perceived consequences of any event come right away. Where sequences are loose, there is a greater interval between events and their perceived consequences. First, let us look at tight sequentiality, then at loose sequentiality.

If I ask a patient, "What are you doing?" and she says, "I'm tapping my foot." and then I ask immediately, "How does that feel?" and she says, "I feel impatient," then I ask immediately again, "What are you doing now?" and she says, "I am tapping harder"— that is tight sequentiality. If I continue in this mode my patient has little chance for pause; taking personal inventory is difficult, and the opportunity for leisurely thoughts and sensations is absent. I am holding her to it, controlling the nature of the sequences so that one experience runs right into another and discrete units lose their identity. It is like a third degree, differing only in the fact that I am not harsh and I am rooting for the patient, who is pressed into a guileless succession of awarenesses. Since there is little room for the events to have understandable implications, the patient may be swept into simple honesty. Faithfulness to her total interests gets lost in a series of reflexive reactions, occurring in a truncated world. The effect is a sharply directed concentration, much as we see in hypnosis or meditation.

All therapies, intentionally or not, set the stage for tightening up the sequences of experience. There is, first of all, an incisive focus by the therapist, who is all eyes and ears. Since there is no telling when the anxiously hidden will appear, the stakes are high. Commentary by the therapist will amplify what the patient has already said and often imply that there is more going on than the patient has revealed. Instructions or implications calling for new or feared behavior will quicken the pulse. At any point the patient's self-concept may be drastically altered; a kind person may discover she is also cruel, an honest person devious, a confident person blowing hot air. The anxiety can accordingly be huge in this struggle between the selectively opaque patient and the seemingly psychic therapist. There is no place to hide.

Here is one example of such therapeutically tight sequentiality. In a therapy workshop, Renata, a woman who doesn't recognize her own compelling presence, complained that she makes herself uninteresting by apologizing a lot and minimizing what she does. She wants to be able to let her words stand on their own, rather than trying to manage people's impressions of her. While she was talking she was reflexively flicking her tongue out. I asked her to notice her tongue and to tell me how it felt. When so ordinarily inconsequential an act as flicking one's tongue out is called to attention, it gives the message that anything could be important and raises alertness. The nonlinear aspect — she didn't know where the question came from — also created disorientation. For a moment, her tongue was all that counted. Furthermore, I suspected there were hidden implications to this movement; the more truth in that suspicion, the more powerful this simple focus would become. With all these factors affecting the split second, she said with wide eyes that her tongue felt wet. Immediately, I pointed out that she said "wet" as though it were the great phenomenon of the world. Then I asked her to flick her tongue out again. She did but this time she felt it stopped her expressiveness. I asked her what made it feel like a blocked expression. She said when she stuck her tongue out the muscles in her face felt constricted.

And so it went, step by step, focusing pointedly on each moment of experience, highlighting what in looser conversation would rarely be given attention. As she went along, continuing the focus on each moment of experience and describing her awareness of it, she began to tremble, more in anger than in sadness or fear. She said there was a frustrating contradiction. On the one hand, she felt an inexplicably stubborn resolve to say nothing, yet she also simultaneously wanted to go on talking. She said that she didn't know the right thing to say. When I asked her to imagine who would know, she said it was the "grownups" who would decide.

Then she became aware that when her tongue flicked out she felt like she was trying to taste and explore the world, a venture of which the "grownups" would strongly disapprove. When I asked her to flick her tongue out anyway, exploring the room as she wished, she felt quite free to do it and was surprised at her own comfort. Soon, however, the stakes increased, because people had become unexpectedly very interested in her; one man, amazingly, even said he was falling in love with her. She felt like she was an "occasion" and continued for a short while playfully to experience her centrality.

After a pleasurable stretch, her mood changed again. Although she wanted no longer to minimize herself, now that she was maximized, being the center of attention apparently disquieted her.

She became scared that she might rise like a balloon and never return to earth. She connected this feeling to her distant childhood, to a fear that someone would get hurt if she remained "up there" and didn't do what she was supposed to. She felt an ominous responsibility—but for what? This dread was maddening. Soon she began agitatedly to cry. When she finished crying she felt like she had at last "come down." Although she felt a little sad about coming down, she discovered that, through the natural release experienced in crying, she was able to survive what momentarily seemed unsurvivable. We can hope that with each new experience of her importance she will be able to feel exhilaration without the prospects of impotent responsibility.

Now let us turn to loose sequentiality, where urgency is often reduced and proportion is restored between any one event and the larger frame into which it fits. Without loose sequentiality all the intense and illuminating experience evolving from tight sequentiality may prove sterile. Consider five of the benefits offered by loose sequentiality: (1) ordinariness, (2) preparation, (3) thinking, (4) assimilation, and (5) opportunity.

(1) Ordinariness is simple respect for unstudied human engagement, where natural sequences unfold with a minimum of management. A person will say in therapy what might be said to a friend, to the family, to a colleague, to someone at a party or in the locker room at the YMCA. Such ordinary talk helps bridge the distance between therapy and "real life." With the mystique of therapy reduced, the range of topics increases and people may more readily experience the conversation as their own.

For example, one of my patients had a lot of money invested in copper. The price had gone damagingly low, so low that even his own large reservoir of money was drying up. He explained to me in great detail the workings of the market pertaining to copper, particularly the fluctuations that have historically marked copper values. He talked about the relationship of copper values to gold and silver values and to the value of the dollar. He spoke also about copper inventory levels and about the industrial uses of copper.

This man was obviously not going to get any financially sophisticated ideas from me; he was teaching me about copper investment as he talked about what was on his mind. My questions and comments were just those of a neophyte talking to an experienced man. Yet he was much relieved by the time he was done. By skillfully voicing his knowledge he confirmed his expertise and his self-esteem rose to its ordinary level, stock market threats notwithstanding. A bonus in this loosely sequenced conversation was that he realized a need for friendship, which he has set aside after relocating in San Diego.

(2) The second contribution of loose sequentiality is preparation. To many unschooled patients simple questions or interpretations, commonly posed by therapists to their therapeutically sophisticated patients, will be confusing or irrelevant. Even so simple a question as "What are you feeling now?" may seem ambiguous, at best, or invasive at worst. One may well wonder why the therapist asks that question or what kind of feelings the therapist is referring to or whether she is asking about a sensation, an emotion, or an attitude. Unless the basis for the question is already apparent in the therapy context, the therapist needs to prepare the ground for inexperienced patients. The therapist might say, "You have a brand-new look on your face, a look I've never seen before. I wonder what you are feeling." The patient will then be more likely to answer, since the transition between the therapist's perception and what she is asking is clarified. Without such preparation, patients may not be able to talk about feelings, or they may do so but with a slave mentality, doing anything that seems called for by the authority.

If I, for example, want a patient to talk to his father, empty chair style, imagining him to be sitting in the room, I must take into account the fact that this patient may be unaccustomed, perhaps reluctant, to talk to people who are not there. He may be using good sense not to do what he doesn't feel right doing. If I nevertheless believe it important that he speak to his father in the empty chair, I may say to him: "Let me tell you what I'd like you to do. It may seem strange to you to do this, but I have found it valuable. Your father is not here. I know, and I think you know, there are certain things you want to say to him. I don't think you can just think about it all in your head and I can't ask you just the right questions to get it out now. I think it will help if you imagine your father is sitting in that chair and just talk to him, just the way you want to."

Such preparation may create the necessary transitional experience. Perhaps he will be unwilling to do it anyway, feeling foolish or frightened. Even so, this experience may pave the way for another one two weeks later. Other preparations may help right away. I may suggest that I do it first. If I already have enough sanity credits with him, this would be all right. He says, "OK, do it." So I talk to my father—or his, if the circumstances favor it. Five minutes go by and he is talking to his father—saying what is on his mind. By this time, with transitional experience preparing the way, he is more likely to be acting out of his integrity than out of obedience to my instruction.

There is, of course, a huge range in the need for preparation. The most courageous or confident or experienced people will not need extensive guidelines and assurances. The therapist must be open to permitting large leaps by those who are capable. But, like a house painter preparing his walls and brushes before painting, the therapist must ready his patients for the procedures he uses.

(3) The third benefit of loose sequentiality is that it leaves room for thinking, for trying out ideas without getting swept along by them. Time for thinking is to the patient as rehearsal time is to the actor or a room of one's own to the writer. It is a luxury of the interior, requiring neither self-commitment nor response from the world. In the privacy of thought the person may wonder why she wants to stay married, whether it is best to take a new job offer, what her friends are doing when she is not with them.

Because it is often substituted for feeling or acting, thinking has received a bad reputation in many psychological circles. However, when it is used for orientation, linking events to one another, it serves to slow down what can't be handled by rapid reflex. It provides a sense of proportion, allowing a bird's-eye view of an enlarged part of the total picture. While thinking often slows a person's pace and moderates excitement, this change of pace may be preparation for new developments.

(4) Assimilation, the fourth element, refers to the individual's allowing things to soak in and become a natural part of her behavior. Something which is revealed in the heat of the moment must

be experienced over and over before it becomes second nature. For example, a woman may find it difficult enough to be assertive in the safety of the therapy room. This is certainly not in the same league as actually reminding her boss that she was not hired to run menial errands. The skills, confidence, and good judgment required for such confrontations are not licensed by a single success in a therapy session. The first time the patient says something to her boss, she may be awkward. After some success, she may be more graceful. Then one day it may no longer be necessary to press her assertiveness, knowing that it will be there when needed.

(5) The fifth factor, opportunity, is often overlooked as an important ingredient in any person's growth. In psychological circles it is commonly thought that opportunities abound in life and that once patients become free-minded these opportunities will be recognized and exploited. Although there is an important element of truth in this belief, the world does not fall easily into place, even if the individual is personally ready. Schools start only once a year, people die any time at all, families are geographically split, stock markets are not responsive to most individuals, people-to-love appear only sporadically, etc. A psychological advance might, therefore, take six months to pay off, as readiness alertly waits for suitable opportunity.

One does not just *wait* for opportunity of course, but since it is not always at hand one can only do the immediately possible and be ready for the harvest when it comes. Although readiness is, indeed, a magnet for opportunity, calling forth unforeseen events, it is not the whole story. Both patient and therapist must be sensitive to the right timing. A person ready for college may have to support her family and so be unable immediately to go. A woman newly confident with men will not necessarily find one on her doorstep. A person primed to switch jobs may have to stay until a new one appears.

Nature does not distribute its generosity evenly. A sensitive loosening of requirements for what-follows-what or how-things-must-happen will give the unequal distribution of opportunity a chance to right itself. With openmindedness and time on one's side the odds on making a good life increase greatly. But in the final analysis one must, indeed, be lucky as well as good.

Always, a person's life is made up of both tight and loose sequentiality. People tailor their lives to include apt proportions of the two styles. One woman, for example, living for years in Los Angeles, bought a house in the country, declaring she no longer wanted to live in the fast lane, where everything mattered too much and right away. If she didn't slam her brakes on at the right moment, her whole life would be changed. If she said the wrong thing at work, she might get fired; conversely, the right thing would get her a promotion. She felt she had to be "on" too much of the time. For her the pressure of tight sequentiality was oppressive. Yet when circumstances are so sterile as to provide little interest in what is next, the individual is sorely challenged to live a workable life. Where, for one horrible example, getting out of prison ten years from now is all that counts, the sequentiality has indeed become torturously loose. A less drastically loose environment is evident in certain small towns, where people are jokingly said to get their entertainment watching the paint dry. In our society people often shift their preferences between the pastoral scene, where they feel they can retreat into a casual relationship of one moment to the next, and the urban throb, where successes sought and opportunities bungled are part of every day's scorecard. It seems fair to say that for many people, happiness will depend on just such choices, as they pace themselves through the continuous sequences of life.

The experience of transition, a simple movement through time, easily eludes people as they cope with complex daily requirements. Yet since nothing stays still, except as we may imagine it, we all live at the transition point between now and next. It is through this movement that people stay fresh and through it that the stories of our lives grow. The therapist, as well as the novelist, attends to the recognition and enhancement of this inevitable movement, even when his patient may not yet see it.

FOUR

Mining for Stories

> Everything in the mind is in rat's country. It doesn't
> die. They are merely carried, these disparate memories,
> back and forth in the desert of a billion neurons, set
> down, picked up and dropped again. . . . You will only
> find the bits and cry out because they were yourself.
>
> —Loren Eiseley
> *All the Strange Hours*

STORIES SEEM surprisingly dangerous to many of the people who might tell them. In fact, the therapist will often have a mind-bending job trying to draw out the ones that actually count. On easy days these stories may be readily apparent and one may gather them like stones off the ground, but at other times they are deeply embedded in their host's psyche. Since the therapist is usually empathic with his patient's experiences and welcomes his accounts, the actual external threat is minimal. But there is an internal threat in each person which sometimes makes the telling of stories forbidding.

An important source of this internal threat is the extra stimulation that comes with the telling of certain highly charged stories. A physically abused person, for example, may feel like a coward for having submitted to beatings by his father, or like a mischief maker for having aroused those beatings, or like a betrayer of his father whom he also has loved, or like a murderer because he wants to kill him. The person may feel that if he tells his story he will erupt, crying uncontrollably or screaming or bursting wide open. When these risks are felt, the stories may remain hidden unless the therapist uses sensitivity and invention to recognize their existence and loosen the right ones. These life-lighting stories are always there, waiting for the right inspiration to bring them out into the open.

The internal threat is not the only barrier to storytelling. People are also overwhelmed by the problem of extracting a simple account of something that matters out of a universe of gradual developments. In a sense, life goes by very slowly while stories—even the longest novels—are quick. The story is an organizing agent, selecting a few events from the many which happen and giving them coherence. One asks, "What did you do today?" and you answer, "I worked all day." This is a meager summary of a day on which you have awakened, conversed with your wife, read many items in the newspaper, had uncountable thoughts, talked to many people about a wide range of topics, remembered past experiences, set up future prospects, felt disappointment, relief, anger and hope, fantasized, eaten, driven your car, etc. "I worked all day" is only the title, a poor one at that, introducing what may actually be a vibrant account. Suppose that during this day, you and a co-worker discussed possibilities for jointly opening your own business. That may stand out from all the day's events and set the theme for the story. The new title, *Moving On*, makes a selection from the events and summarizes what is to be elaborated.

The novelist is better known than the therapist for extracting a story line from a medley of actual experiences. Proust's narrator in his *Remembrance of Things Past* says that he fell in love with the novel when, as a boy, he discovered the dramatic clarity with which it condensed a lifetime. For him, the novel speeded up life's process, replacing gradualism with a quick "mental picture." Through ingenious acceleration of events, the novelist crams his pages with "more dramatic and sensational events than occur, often, in a lifetime." Even with the novel, however, the reader must remain attentive to the gradual development of story line, staying focused on the details and alert for the advances in plot. So also from the agglomeration of detail in everyday life, one must condense all the events into a coherent unit, lively and reportable.

Needing to summarize what takes too much time, energy and memory to report, people will choose *titles* to serve as pointers toward events long ago locked away yet still anxiously leaning toward awareness. These titles are often substitutes rather than introductions to the experiences they point to. In fiction, a title without a story would be absurd, only a starting point; however, in life people commonly accept the titles to their stories without looking closely to see how these match the actual experiences.

One woman, about to marry but worried because she had previously shown poor judgment about men, saw herself as having had a terrible sexual relationship with her ex-husband. However, she could at first tell me little about it. All she would say was that she had a *Terrible Sexual Relationship*—only a title, but one from which she could not escape as long as the actual details were missing. As we talked further, it became clear to her that she could say much more. Oddly, she hadn't before realized that the events were worth telling. She told me that her husband would watch Playboy TV night in and night out, no longer interested in her. He had herpes and was sexually contagious two weeks out of four. Not only was he contagious much of the time but he wouldn't tell her when he was contagious, so she had to be personally on the lookout for it. Her *Terrible Sexual Relationship*, now more than a title, evolved into a convincing tale of misery.

This woman's current man was everything her ex-husband wasn't—considerate, accomplished, admiring, open, and easily sexual. But the title of her story was so heavily imprinted in her mind that she had been unable to set her past relationship into its historic place and trust the new one. In telling the details that made up the substance of *Terrible Sexual Relationship*—or*Abusive Men*— and in telling the details of her new relationship, she imbued each with greater reality. Without this substantiality, all relationships with men were identified with a label rolling free in her head, unaffected by changes in her actual experience. She was living a new story with the same old title. As long as her title was isolated from its story, the truth of her new experiences was as dependable as a mirage. Any trustworthy change in self-image calls for the new experiences to be psychologically registered. Otherwise, looking for one's actuality—Can I trust my judgment about men?—is like a shell game in which the pea is never there.

The function of connecting the title with the story goes beyond catharsis, through which people are freed of whatever is caught inside them, or insight, through which people understand themselves. People often summarize the events of their lives in a word or two and then forget what it is they have summarized. At first, the special titles they give themselves are convenient symbols or guides in an otherwise incomprehensible existence. But the details, the substance of life, may be lost. When the story is told again and substance and title connected, congruence is restored and a sense of wholeness regained.

This integration of title and event is an indispensable condition for grounded living. For someone to say he is "country folk," for example, is not the same as giving a description of the Baptist revivalist meetings he attended, the games he and his friends played, the whippings he suffered, or the panic he felt getting lost in the city. Patients who come for therapy present their problems as abstractions, such as "marital troubles," "homosexuality," "school failure," or "fear of elevators." These titles crowd their minds, leaving only a little room for the unique elaborations peculiar to each person. Once the unique quality is restored, the titles may change—and their lives, too. "Marital discord" may become "boiling in the kitchen" or the "homosexual life" may become "better than to be a boxer." Still, no matter how intriguing the new titles may be, or how reorienting, they can never substitute for the story itself.

The sterility of substituting titles for details was illustrated by Director Mike Nichols in an interview with Barbara Gelb. He described an experience while he was a student in Lee Strasberg's class at the Actors Studio. Two actors were playing out a love scene. When Strasberg asked the woman what she was doing to bring on the desired emotion, she said she thought of the ordinary things—the spring, longing, loving—all empty of detail. All Strasberg wanted to know, he said, was whether she knew how to make a fruit salad. She was confused about the question but told him how she would do it. "I take an apple and I peel it and I cut it into slices. Then I peel an orange and cut it into slices. Maybe I take a few cherries and pit them and cut them into slices. And then I mix it all together." Strasberg then said, "That's right, that's how you make a fruit salad, and until you pick up each piece of fruit, one at a time, peel it, and cut it into slices, you don't have fruit salad. You can run over the fruit with a steam roller, but you won't have fruit salad. Or you can sit in front of the fruit all night, saying, 'OK, fruit salad.' Nothing will happen, though, until you pick up each piece and peel it and cut it up." We are all vulnerable to empty function, playing the abstract themes without the substance out of which they are composed.

ASKING QUESTIONS

A time-honored way to give flesh to implied events is to ask the questions that will call elaborations to mind. These questions must come from an abiding curiosity and an intent to create wholeness and color. If I ask whether you have any brothers or sisters, you may answer either generously or meagerly, according to the way I ask or when I ask. In many interviews all the questioner wants to know is the simple, direct answer to the question, period. However, to pose the question as an invitation to reveal oneself opens up each person's unique options.

Questions do not have to be as dramatic as, "Did you ever want to kill your father?" although such queries may, on occasion, be rightly evocative. They may proceed step-by-step, building up a natural momentum and emphasizing each moment's implications for the next. This gradual process helps a person to experience his own initiative and to retain control over the movement toward climactic clarity. Suppose I ask my patient if he has a brother.

"Yes."

"Where does he live?"

"In Connecticut."

"He's very far away, isn't he?"

"Yes, I see him only now and then."

"Do you miss him?"

"Yes, he is a good person to talk to and we *now* talk very well together." (Hint of previous trouble)

"Has it always been that way?"

"No, I used to be very scared of him. He was older and stronger than me. I once saw him beat up a neighborhood kid. People pulled him off. The kid was bleeding bad; people had to pull my brother off. I found out later the kid had called my mother a whore. She was separated from my father and there were some men who had come to visit. But I didn't know that and I made it my business to stay away from my brother."

And so the story goes.

In this example the story line gradually gathers a force of its own, heading toward greater detail as tensions are revealed, confusions implied, changes uncovered, violence threatened, and resolutions promised. The piggy-backing bits and pieces fill out the experience of this person's life—and the therapist's experience, too. The progression happens with only the slightest guidance, at first a step at a time, until the details gain momentum, speeding up everything that is recounted.

Actor Ralph Richardson in an interview with Benedict Nightingale, speaks of a similar exploratory inquiry in preparing for parts. He says, "Dig, dig, dig, dig. Find out more about the character. What does he eat? What trousers does he wear? What does he drink? What is he afraid of? All these things and more you've got to know. And you add to that rags and tags, chance conversations you hear, people you see walking down the street, anything that might fit the part."

One example of just such a digging process, a gentle one, is the step-by-step elaboration of a story line through sensitive questioning in the session described below. Clara was a 40-year-old Italian woman who as a child had been raped by an American soldier. She had been unable to encompass the horror of this event; it was so alien to her sense of being that she had not even brought it up in a previous psychoanalysis. The session was a part of a group therapy experience led by me as part of a month-long training program in gestalt therapy. It was conducted by one of the trainees, Marilyn Blank.

As the session began Clara informed the group that, after hearing Marilyn describe her work with rape victims, she had decided she wanted to work with her about her rape experience. Marilyn agreed and they proceeded within the therapy group, which had been meeting daily as part of the training format. Through gentle and sensitive questions, Marilyn drew out the story of Clara's experience, going beyond the title of *Rape* by harvesting many details and their accompanying feelings. The story moved gradually through sequences of Clara's innocence, her generosity, her experience of invasion, and her horror. It brought relief and substantiation of a part of Clara's life, horrible events which had previously caused her to feel alienated and tainted.

Although the account of this session is lengthy, it is worth relating in detail to get across the power of the gradual movement from the abstraction "rape" to the concrete events which gave palpability to this compelling human story. At first, earlier in the session than reported here,* Marilyn created a sense of mutual interest and support, set the stage for their work, and asked questions which evoked awareness in Clara of her tight throat, of the experience of blushing and stroking her neck when using the word "rape," and of her changes in breathing and voice tone. She described the town where she lived as a child, how she played with her friends, and how she wore her hair. When the day of the rape came into the picture, we in the group were already involved and could identify with Clara's life.

The following dialogue between Marilyn and Clara formed the heart of her story. Marilyn's questions, as will be evident, continued to evoke both the detail and the inevitably ensuing drama, neither she nor Clara digressing into abstractions.

MARILYN: Can you remember what you did when you were alone that afternoon [the day of the rape]?
CLARA: Yes, oh yes. I walked away from the village square that day and walked to a small wooden bridge outside of town that was built over a brook. The brook had the same name as the town I lived in. The bridge went over the water and I loved to sit there and hang my feet into the water, especially on hot days. I was also very careful not to wet my dress. That made my mother angry. During the war we had few dresses.
MARILYN: Do you know why that bridge was there?

---

*This is as close to a verbatim account as Marilyn could produce right after the session. To me, it seems quite faithful to the actual words.

CLARA: The cows used that bridge to walk to the nearby meadows. Every afternoon that I played there I could touch the cows as they passed by. But this afternoon it was very quiet and it felt good to dangle my feet in the brook. (Broad smile)

MARILYN: Do you remember what happened next? You were sitting on the bridge alone with your feet dangling off the edge into the brook, and . . .

CLARA: There were loud, heavy footsteps coming towards me. The village people didn't have heavy leather shoes; there was a shortage of leather during the war. When I looked up all I could see were big, black, heavy army boots and an olive green uniform. I remember that the leather shoes went half-way up his legs. I never saw this before.

MARILYN: What else can you remember noticing about these shoes as you sat there on the bridge, dangling your feet in the water?

CLARA: It was not common in Italy to see shoes, especially leather shoes that tied halfway up anyone's legs. These black boots had many laces and I think they were shiny. They looked so big to me. The soldier was tall, very tall, with dark olive skin and dark hair.

MARILYN: Was he a black man?

CLARA: Oh no, he just had very dark olive skin.

MARILYN: Can you remember what he first said or did?

CLARA: He smiled, yes, he smiled and then sat down next to me and put his army boots into the water and he did just what I was doing. I thought this was very strange to put your feet in the water with boots on. (A childlike quality enters her voice and face — innocence personified.)

MARILYN: I would imagine that he looked strange doing this alongside of you. What happened next?

CLARA: Yes, he did. After a few minutes passed he offered me chewing gum. This was the second time in my life I ever had gum. At first I didn't know what to do with it, so I sucked on it. Then he showed me how to chew on it and not suck on it.

MARILYN: Can you remember what you were feeling?

CLARA: Yes, he seemed so friendly and happy just to be sitting there with me and both our feet in the brook. I felt happy.

MARILYN: Did you stay there very long with him?

CLARA: No, because he asked me to show him the way to a neighboring village and he told me that he wanted to go by way of the railroad tracks.

MARILYN: Could you understand him?

CLARA: We didn't speak the same language, but with the help of hand gestures I understood what he wanted and thought to myself that his request to walk along the direction of the railroad tracks was unusual. Yes, an unusual way to get to the next town. The train only went by twice a day in the summer and many of the townspeople and soldiers used the train tracks as a street.

MARILYN: How well you remember this day.

CLARA: I am surprised.

MARILYN: Did you offer him directions?

CLARA: Yes, but he asked me to show him the way and I said I would. I remember he helped me up off the bridge and my feet left the water. We walked through the village square together, like old friends would walk.

MARILYN: Did townspeople see you both?

CLARA: Oh yes, we walked so all could see.

MARILYN: How long was the walk?

CLARA: It was about one mile through the village and one and a half miles in the direction of the neighboring village.

MARILYN: Did you stop along the way?

CLARA: Yes, after walking about one and a half miles he stopped to take a break. He sat down along the side of the train tracks on a small hill and gestured for me to sit down next to him.

MARILYN: Did you?

CLARA: Oh yes. After I sat down he pulled out a bar of chocolate candy and gave it to me. It was the first bar of chocolate I ever saw. I remember wanting to save it so I could take it home to share with my mother and brother. I didn't want to open it but he insisted that I eat it. I remember him taking my hands and forcing me to open the candy bar and eat it. I didn't understand this and I felt a little scared. But I wanted to please him. He smiled when I took my first bite and I thought I made him happy. He insisted I take a second bite and insisted I eat the whole bar of chocolate, even though my mouth was full. He insisted I continue chewing and didn't stop until I took the rest of the chocolate in my mouth. He made me quickly eat the whole thing. It was too much candy and I had a difficult time swallowing such big pieces of candy. But he wouldn't let me stop.

MARILYN: You must have been confused by his behavior.

CLARA: Oh, I was, and soon after I finished the candy bar he suddenly changed. You know, I felt so guilty eating the whole candy bar. I so wanted to bring it home to my family. I wanted to surprise them. But he didn't understand that.

As his manner changed, so too did his voice. It grew rougher to me. He stopped smiling and suddenly pulled me into the bushes and pushed me down on the ground. I remember feeling a rock in my back as he pushed me down. The harder he pushed the more the rock pushed into my back against me. The rock was shaped like a point and it was terrible. You know, it just pressed into my back. I remember the earth under me. I remember lying on the slope with a rock pressing in my back.

MARILYN: I am beginning to feel the struggle you describe. Take as much time as you need before telling what happened next.

CLARA: Oh, I will. I can still feel the rock pressing on my back, and oh yes, I remember I had to pee, but he wouldn't let me get up and it was so hard to move away. He pushed me down again and pulled off my underpants and threw them down the slope. (A long pause)

You know, I was so scared I couldn't hold my bladder and I remember my pee running out and running down the slope on the hill onto my underpants. That was the worst for me. I was afraid that my mother would find out and be angry with me for wetting my pants. I only owned two pairs of underpants.

MARILYN: You were such a proud little girl. How helpless and scared you must have felt.

CLARA: I was scared of him and scared of ruining my underpants and dress.

MARILYN: Can you slowly begin to remember what happened next?

CLARA: Yes.

MARILYN: Where was the American soldier? What was he saying to you and what was he doing to you? Take all the time you need.

CLARA: OK. (Pause) Next he was all over me. All I could see was an olive green uniform on my face. He became harsher with me, his voice changed, he had his penis out, and I could feel him lift my dress and wet me. He was like a black blob on me and I couldn't see anything and I couldn't breathe. (Clara begins to touch her throat as she experiences the trauma of that event.)

I remember trying to find a space to breathe. I managed to turn my head from side to side to find some air. I used all the strength I had to breathe. I couldn't breathe. I couldn't breathe. Not with that big black blob on me.

MARILYN: Were you able to get the air you needed to breathe?

CLARA: Yes, each time I turned my head to the side I found some air. He was so big, and pushed so hard on me and the rock pushed even harder against my back.

MARILYN: I would like you now to take some time to breathe. Look around and remember to take in all the air you need to breathe. (Practices just breathing for a few minutes)

CLARA: I'm breathing. It was so hard to breathe then and all I could see was olive green and it was like a black cloud came over me.

MARILYN: Can you feel the difference between then and now? That little girl—you—was determined to survive.

CLARA: Oh yes. I'm not wet, there is no stone in my back and he isn't smothering me. (Long pause)

MARILYN: It's important to experience the differences. Can we talk a little more about the rape, right now? And remember to breathe.

CLARA: Yes.

MARILYN: When the soldier was on top of you can you remember if he penetrated you?

CLARA: He tried. There was no bleeding, but I was wet on my vagina from him and from my pee.

MARILYN: Did you cry?

CLARA: Oh no.

MARILYN: You were both so proud and so scared and so able to take care of yourself, even in a crisis.

CLARA: Of course. I was so humiliated.

MARILYN: Can you remember when he left you?

CLARA: Yes, all of a sudden he jumped off me, closed his pants and left. When I got up, I saw that my hands had dirt on them, because I was holding onto the ground so tightly. I walked down the slope and picked up my pants and quickly put them on, wet, and then I ran through the meadow to my favorite hiding place along the brook.

MARILYN: The cows' meadows . . .

CLARA: Yes. (Smiling)

MARILYN: Did anyone see you as you ran through the meadows?

CLARA: No. I ran through sight unseen. I made certain that no one saw me. You know, I would have jumped fences in order to get there the back way so that I would not be seen.

MARILYN: Remember to take time to breathe.

CLARA: Yes.

MARILYN: What did you do when you got there?

CLARA: I sat down by the brook, took off my underpants and washed them. They were wet and stained with earth and leaves. I wiped off my dress and cleaned myself.

MARILYN: How long were you there?

CLARA: I stayed there until it was dark and then walked home.

MARILYN: Do you remember why you waited so long to go home?

CLARA: I didn't want to see anyone — any adult. And if I walked home in the dark no one could see the dirt stains on my dress.

MARILYN: You were a brave child and so willing to keep this event away from your family.

CLARA: Oh yes, I had to, my mother had so many problems from the war.

MARILYN: Can you remember walking into your home that night?

CLARA: Oh yes, I remember walking through the village square and I remember entering the house. First I did my chores and then I sat down with my family to dinner.

MARILYN: Did your mother ask you any questions about your dress or underpants?

CLARA: Oh no, I made certain that my dress covered my underpants.

MARILYN: I want you to know that I believe your story and every detail you stated. (Marilyn's hand is touching Clara's knee. Clara looks surprised and relieved)

CLARA: You do?

MARILYN: Oh yes, and I appreciate how well you took care of yourself that day. You also showed so much sensitivity to your family. Did you or one of them mention it at all that night?

CLARA: No. Absolutely no.

MARILYN: So you sat there all alone at the dinner table with your pain and your story.

CLARA: Yes.

MARILYN: (Touching her hand) You were such a lovely child, so brave, so special. (Both smile.) I would like to stop here. I think we are finished for now.

CLARA: So do I. You know, this wasn't as scary remembering as I thought it would be.

MARILYN: What have you been remembering with me today?

CLARA: The rape when I was a child.

MARILYN: Breathe for a few seconds. Just take in some breaths and when you are ready make contact again with the group.

What was central to this session was the movement the questions created in bringing a muffled event to life. Through this transformation, we were led to experience not only a rape but a particular rape of a particular person. The theme guided us to many special experiences — the arresting symbol of a forced chocolate bar, an endearing dread of wet pants, a hard rock in the back, an uncomprehending terror. *Rape* as a title pointed us toward the story in all its dimensions. With that accomplished, the title was no longer merely a label.

In questioning patients, the therapist is not limited to narrow step-by-step questions and will sometimes ask those with larger compass. He may ask people about a time in their lives when their survival was at stake, about a memorable person, about an event that mystified them, a time of rejuvenation or helplessness, a rescue, a time when they saw someone dead, a firsthand burglary, an exciting date, leaving home for the first time, and so forth. These are universal themes; questions concerning them spark stories flavored by the unique experiences of any person's life.

More individualized questions may be directly connected to what is already going on. One woman, for example, was huddled in her chair, with her jacket on as though for warmth. I asked her *how old* she felt. She said she felt like ten and then went into an extended account of a time, at ten, when her father had taken her to a bar. For the first time she was able to say how incredibly special she felt when he took her there and how this feeling contrasted with her disgust and frustration with him and the ugliness of their relationship. A macho man, he had repeatedly degraded her, even though he alternately treated her as special. She had come to discount the special, and although she had all the earmarks of a special person — bright, talented, sensitive — she had blunted her specialness. Through telling her story, she saw that, in spite of some contrary indications, her father actually did find her special. She further realized that friends, teacher, and husband could also find her special.

EVERY WHOLE HAS ITS PARTS

A variation on the theme of transforming the abstract into the specific is played out in the reverberations between the whole of any experience and its ingredients. The whole is not necessarily an abstraction. To say, for example, in response to an offer of a cigarette, "I don't want one," is a specific statement that can stand all by itself. Yet, contained within the simple wholeness of this response are many ingredients, which might be extracted and elaborated. Did you give up smoking? If so, what kind of struggle was it? Is smoking morally repugnant? Do you feel fresher since quitting? Are you nervous? Do you breathe differently? Are you proud? Are you lonely? Were you forbidden to smoke at 14? Any experience contains a supply of stories.

In giving depth to events, the novelist takes special advantage of whole and ingredient experiences, sometimes even when the events seem mundane. A special way of saying "yes," for example, may imply "at last"; a pause in a conversation may indicate trepidation; a car won't start and one will be late again; the dry cleaner loses a favorite dress: all will serve as keys to story material. These events may all be ingredients of the same whole experience — poor-self esteem, for example. Or they may be wholes themselves, each calling for further details. Any experience is like a box within a box, each containing a box while being contained within one.

The natural fluctuations of attention between the whole and its ingredients engender increased energy. In cubist painting, for example, energy is derived from the breakup of the intended whole image into parts which are not placed to fit clearly into a recognizable whole. When the viewer is able to see the splits — nose, face, and legs going off at different angles — and then to recompose the whole through his own synthesizing process, he may find this construction exciting. In a sense he and the painter have both created the painting. As E. H. Gombrich has said in *The Story of Art*, this "can be done only with more or less familiar forms. Those who look at the picture (violin) must know what a violin looks like to be able to relate the various fragments in the picture to each other. That is why Cubist painters usually choose familiar motifs . . . where we can easily pick our way through the painting and understand the relationship of the various parts." Likewise it is necessary to retain a sense of the recomposable whole when breaking down any experience — such as one's specialness — into a mosaic of events contained within it.

Relationships between wholes and their ingredients suffer the same disconnections that repression creates between the conscious and unconscious. Repression has long been recognized as a major source of the loss of personal ingredients and of deficits in energy and function. Through the recognition of the unconscious and its repression, depth and variety have been revealed in even the simplest human experience. But the concept of *ingredients* differs from that of unconscious. Ingredients are simply elements — not causes — in a detailed composition. Some are well within the range of conscious awareness. Until attention is called to them they may be considered unimportant, irrelevant, or untimely, even though they are readily describable. If, for example, I point out to a patient who has been speaking with a tightly controlled chest that he just took a deep breath, he may already know this. But he may not include it as a party to his experience. Once he notices the breath and sees it as relevant, he may return to the conversation more wholeheartedly.

Fleshing Out a Flash

The writer has much greater opportunity than the therapist to expand a flash of experience into a rich composition. A moment's thought, a fleeting image, or a passing sensation in real life can be extended into pages of text. The novelist can interrupt any sequence of actions — with elaborations of his character's internal process, with past events which explain current activity, or even with a digression from the narrative by the author himself. The fertile detour is well traveled. Although these detours are more difficult in either therapy or everyday conversation, we can all learn from the novelist how to use them.

An illustration of fleshing out a flash is given in William Styron's *Sophie's Choice*. Styron populates a moment between one sentence of a conversation and the next with a string of ruminations. Stingo, a 22-year-old budding writer, is in love with Sophie, a slightly older woman of great beauty. She, however, is in love with Nathan, also a dear friend of Stingo's, so he has kept his romantic dreams private. As luck would have it, his friends fight, as they do periodically. But this time their relationship has developed a serious crack. Stingo and Sophie retreat together to a beach, privately. They are naked. In the heat of the moment and in his virginal state he suffers the rotten fate of a premature ejaculation. This is no problem to Sophie, who surmises him to be a virgin anyway, has no stake in his performance, and loves him notwithstanding his anxious sexuality. He groans his confession of virginity. At that moment of mortification she tells him how much he is like Josef, a long ago lover in Poland who had been killed by the Nazis.

She goes on to talk about Josef — the mystery of his death, the picnics they went on, and the difficulties during the war. Stingo is astounded that she can go on this way. Between one of Sophie's sentences and the next he interpolates a rush of seriocomic dismay about the incongruence of her rattling on about the distant past while he lies there limp. What seems like his sexual demise is, temporarily at least, the very fulcrum of Stingo's existence. While Sophie talks, a whole page of text detours into silent regions of Stingo's mind.

Although Sophie may be unaware that anything else is happening, we readers know what is going on in Stingo. This reverberation between the surface and the undercurrent gives the experience depth. Yet in real life the accessibility of the often unruly details depends so much on good timing and mutuality that it is very limited. If Stingo's asides had actually been inserted into the dialogue, rather than recorded inaudibly in his own mind, it would surely have changed his engagement with Sophie. Had he said out loud what only he and the reader are privy to, Sophie would have been brought into a new contact with him and might have been drawn away from her own need to reminisce about Josef. Maybe that would have been better for her. Maybe it would have given Stingo greater leverage and self-respect if he had forced her to pay attention to his dismay rather than to the long gone Josef. We may all only speculate about that. Nevertheless, it is clear that to verbalize the unraveling of his mind Stingo would have required greater than ordinary freedom.

In therapy, the opportunities for fleshing out a flash are better than in everyday life though not as great as in a novel. One is less restricted to the requirements of purpose, linear continuity, and contact between people and may instead hunt for the ingredients of any experience. This exploratory freedom is illustrated by therapeutic working-through with Iris. She experienced an inexplicable shortfall in her relationships with other members of a therapy group. The "click" was missing. A sense of disconnection between her and them persisted in spite of many warm exchanges. People told her they liked her rapt attention, how she seemed to understand what people were talking about, how very special her kind of attractiveness was — not beautiful but she was a pleasure to look at. Iris accentuated her normally squared look, pondered the words she had heard, and then said defensively, "What do you mean, *not beautiful?*" This simple remark, a flash of expression, could easily have slid by, as most flashes do. But Iris' attention to the undercurrents of "not beautiful" resulted in a generous account of her concerns with beauty. Her confusion about it was so great that it was never far from her awareness.

Iris' father, a generally kind man, had wanted her to be a beauty queen, as her mother had been. He thought she looked more like him, though, and he had never liked how he looked. Iris, on the other hand, thought she looked terrific, but she wanted *him* to think she was beautiful. He was never able to see it, so they never quite connected. Something was always missing. Finally, Iris banished any wish to be physically beautiful, negated her father's values about beauty and strove to be beautiful "in spirit" instead. Other people's references to physical beauty made her indignant. By the time of this session, only "doing good" mattered. She had turned out to be a harsh judge of others, who by her standards did not "do good," and had succeeded in alienating herself from her own ambitions to be beautiful.

As people in the group continued to refer to her as attractive, Iris found them harder to dismiss. She began to soften and color slightly. When I wondered out loud whether she could contain all she would feel if she felt beautiful, she began to blush. Now she could feel the heat inside and her pleasure with this feeling healed the split she had felt between her and the other people in the group. Her radiance was the light turned on by expanding a flash, *not beautiful*, which contained important elements of the total person she was. Was she beautiful? I thought so and for one moment she did too.

Awarenesses are Signals

Awareness is a simple and fundamental element of human experience. It serves as a signal on simple sensory levels, telling us whether we are warm or cold, frightened or calm, sensually aroused, or physically ill. Or it may serve on a complex level, accenting attitudes about work, city, family, companions, or way of life. Both novelist and therapist are commissioned to help restore awareness where it is missing or to accent awareness so that it becomes an effective and rewarding partner to the actions in anybody's life. They do this through their own devices, each calling attention to the huge range of experiences that people might either overlook or only faintly recognize. Through the heightened awareness, people are enabled to make pointedly personal choices. These choices range all the way from eating only when hungry to selecting a mate or finding work consistent with personal needs. Awareness may be sharp or dull, much as cameras may vary in focus; the sharper the focus, the more dependable the foundation for choice.

Suppose, for example, that in a conversation with a friend a person fails to be aware of the point at which he just gets tired and runs out of talk. Instead of stopping, he goes on, and what had been a good talk winds down to a pointless ending. The two say goodbye at last, feeling vague discomfort. But they ignore this. After all, nobody needs always to be happy. However, they have missed the beat of their awareness. To have recognized and acknowledged fatigue would have been a warm thing to do with a good friend, and if they had both been interested in the one's tiredness (why not?), they would have quit while ahead — or a remark about the fatigue might have led to renewed liveliness. Instead, they maintained pale experience, almost as though by self-negation they were giving one another a gift. Some gift!

Eventually, when the neglect of awareness becomes habitual, it may well deteriorate into opaqueness. Without sharp awareness, people are deprived of a basic affirming function, of a direct recognition of reality. For the novelist, the process of creating this affirmation, this reality, is commonplace. One small example is taken from *Lady Oracle*, a novel written by Margaret Atwood. Joan, the primary character, has to get away. She has arranged her seeming death and escaped from Canada to Italy. She awakes in a small hotel after a night of drinking:

> When I woke up the next morning my euphoria was gone. I didn't exactly have a hangover, but I didn't feel like getting up too suddenly. The Cinzano bottle was standing on the table, empty; what I found ominous about this was that I couldn't remember finishing it. Arthur used to tell me not to drink so much. He wasn't a great drinker himself, but he had a habit of bringing a bottle home from time to time and leaving it out where I could see it. I suppose it was like a kid's chemistry set for him; secretly he liked mixing me up, he knew something exciting would happen. Though he was never sure what, or what he wanted; if I'd known that it would have been easier.

Through paying attention to her awarenesses, Joan not only manifests the otherwise hidden workings of her mind but also is led, as is the reader, beyond her immediate self to a recognition of a number of ingredients of her life: Arthur, wine, secret purposes, forgetfulness, remembering, confusion, hints about trouble, the vagaries of emotion, etc. In just a few words a rich fabric of experience is woven. It's only one paragraph—and perhaps easily forgotten as the story goes on—but the details contribute to all that follows, as each recognition blends into the next and then the next.

Compare Joan's statement to the following from Nancy, a member of a therapy group:

> I'm feeling funny today. Feeling real careful and real cautious. I don't like being where I am at all. Every time I think of working [therapeutically], my heart starts to beat . . . a lot of things come to mind—the onstage feeling I get a lot of times. The person inside me wants to be at home, silly or whatever. The more I talk the scareder I get. It's connected with some unfinished business I have with Tom [a colleague and also a group member, present].

Here there are plenty of hints, not as generously or as palpably stated as with Atwood's Joan, that there are dramatic things going on in Nancy's life. She is too scared to say right off what they are; perhaps she doesn't even know. In the group Nancy goes on to say that because she doesn't feel "important" she's like a little girl and because she is scared she feels "like World War III could happen." These awarenesses would not fly in a novel, nor would these statements themselves lead the group members to care much about Nancy. What saved her was that she was in a firsthand experience with me and other group members and we knew her well. This intimacy made up for her suggestive but undeveloped thoughts and her pounding heart announced vital concerns.

Following her small degree of ventilation, however, Nancy suddenly felt calm. I told her I was sorry she had gotten over her anxiety so quickly because I had expected it would point the way to something vital for her. There had to be more substance to her anxiety. Otherwise, what's all the fuss about? It was like those movies in which the audience hears ominous footsteps approaching a house, and it turns out to be only the paper boy.

Nancy didn't expect this reaction, since she believed people preferred calmness—but it resulted in her taking a second look. She soon expressed disgust as she realized what she had skipped over. She was angry at another group member, Evangeline, who had spoken scathingly about her nextdoor neighbor. Nancy thought it was awful that Evangeline would not be more "understanding." She slammed her as arrogant, then in a moment also accosted Tom for being icy with her. Tom was actually the main event, as foretold in her opening remarks. She wanted him to treat her as an equal, but since he was stiff with her she had been resigned to a disapproving distance between them. She told him that when he got stiff she got stubborn and was unwilling to cooperate with him. Although Nancy was quite anxious again in telling him her feelings, Tom listened with great interest and acknowledged that he disliked her stubbornness. But he never felt he could do anything about it. Now that the ogre was met, Nancy went on to tell him about a dream she had in which they were dancing together in a natural, loving relationship, very simple and very warm. She said she felt no sexual overtones but had been afraid that's what he might think. Instead, she just felt an easy equality with him rather than a devouring sexuality. This time she became calm through success in fully facing Tom rather than through avoidance.

GUIDING IMAGE

Though the experiences of each life are unique, common threads are discernible. These motifs, perhaps never so identifiable in actual life as in novels, are concise clarifications of important areas of experience. Under the best conditions these themes serve as launching points from which therapy will proceed. For example, a clear motif for one patient was his negative language in describing positive experience. Instead of seeing a woman as attractive, he would say she was "not unattractive." Instead of saying he was an excellent lawyer, he would say he was "not bad in comparison with the great ones." Instead of saying he was excited about coming in for his therapy session, he would say he was "not in desperate need." Not surprisingly, he was impotent. The existence of such an organic union between the theme of a person's life — chronic negativity in this case — and his newly discovered problem — impotence — helps the therapist in the guesses he makes about how his patients are running their lives.

The novelist is faithful to this connection, too. If he sees a character as down on his luck, the stories will be quite different from what they would be if he saw the same character as having a stubborn streak. A case in point is John Gardner's account (in *On Becoming a Novelist*) of his guiding image for his novel, *October Light*. He said he wanted to write a novel about the virtues of New England values — "good workmanship, independence, unswerving honesty, and so on." This image served well as long as the behavior fit. However, as Gardner got deeply into the story, he began to see that his characters were no longer behaving as his guiding image would require. Without intention on his part, his characters were becoming vicious. Brothers and sisters were locking each other out of their lives, at one point even trying to maim each other. For Gardner to remain true to the actual course of events, his original guiding image had to yield, in the service of organic unity, to the facts as they developed. Though virtue may have been his starting point, once the events contradicted virtue the guiding image changed to the stubbornness and alienation which accompany self-centered virtue.

One of the primary functions of therapy is to change just such guiding images, those which patients have lived with but which are currently outdated. One example of such a change in guiding image concerns a 35-year-old patient. She was a very energetic, assertive woman, who was also incongruously dependent and anxious. In her need for attention and reassurance, she could be insufferably self-centered. This troublesome combination of dependency and self-centeredness dominated my image of her. One experience in her background stood out. Her father had died suddenly when she was five but, strangely, her family withheld this from her, presumably not to burden her. They told her he was sick, or that he was traveling. Of course, it was impossible to maintain the lie, and although she could not say just how she found out the truth, she stayed confused for a long time.

One day I wrote a sketch of her, much as though I were free

associating, and what I wrote transformed my guiding image. In the sketch, my image of this woman as dependent gave way to seeing her as a devoted, generous hostess, who, following the tone of her family, was psychologically keeping her dead father alive. Here is the sketch, written after some puzzling dream work with her:

> The crud of dream, her past sorrow, lingers in her. The chance for cleansing it appears outside the dream, right in front of her, but her father will not allow this release for he would then disappear into the past, joined with undistinguished dust. Instead he rides parasitically in her head, seemingly pulling the reins, hoping her love would blind her to this incursion. Death coming long ago had changed him, made him resolve to have a familiar, eternal resting place.
>
> He looks warily around, embedded in her head, protruding in her wide eyes, dreading the moment of discovery. She had forgotten that she sustains him there, a hostess to his pulse. She is always seeking his old generous nature, hoping to drown out the now-foul taste in her head. His shame of encroachment has been surrounding him with cautious wall, opaque but crumbling—only barely enfolding her freedom, wanting at last to enter ever, away from his familial prison. The force of their prior union still stands before them, thinking autonomously but now welcoming a change. They need only to look straightaway and see there, where radiance returns to her and rest to him. Then the dream dissolves and life may tide anew.

From this point on, my seeing her as a generous hostess rather than as a dependent narcissist helped create a turn in her story line. From this new perspective, we together took account of her experiences as a social worker, a political activist, and a dependable, though perhaps excessively attentive, friend—all of which expanded the recognition of her generosity and added confirmation of her independent existence. Then the most important realization came. In her relationship to her husband, she was simulating the spurious position of *seeming* to be dependent upon him. Actually, she was continually supporting him. She was able, through a period of agonizing uncertainty, to leave this marriage and proceed forward in the service of her own strong will.

A special form of guiding image is the metaphor, which consolidates much of a person's life into a single, representative picture. This picture will accent a compelling motif and, when timely, release the stories behind the picture. Once, for example, I remarked to a somber yet dashingly mustachioed man, who was wearing a broad-striped shirt, that he reminded me of a burlgar who had just been released from prison and had not yet changed his clothes. He was no burglar, of course. Yet, after a few conversational exchanges, he began to tell me about this old trauma. When he was a child, his father had been tried for the murder of his wife, this man's mother. His father and mother had apparently made a suicide pact, but his father survived. However, the father's story was not accepted, so he was prosecuted on a murder charge, of which he was eventually acquitted. Even though the experiences were dramatically important for this man, without the metaphor evoked by his prison-like shirt the story would likely have remained untold.

Another person in another group was wearing a pure white turban, which rose high above his head. He was a light-complexioned person, with apple cheeks and a boy-next-door look — certainly no one you would expect to see in a turban. In fact, he looked as though he had been captured and placed into the turban. I told him he reminded me of a calf in a rodeo, roped by a huge quantity of rolled white gauze that a cowboy had wound around and around his head. In responding to my metaphor, the young man told us how he had been roped into this Indian religious sect by both his wife and the very dominant and threatening leader of the sect. He had remained because of his wife's devotion to the religious principles but he was now uncertain about remaining.

Curious about how his turban would feel on my head, I asked if I might wear it. He agreed. I liked the feeling of elaborated existence this dome gave me. For him this was an opportunity to try out a short period without the turban. Within a year, not without turmoil, he finally succeeded in breaking away from the religious sect, subsequently achieving successes in the workaday world which had eluded him while he remained roped in.

Some of these metaphorical introductions to story line represent remarkable coincidences between innocently conceived images and pivotal experiences. Some would say that extrasensory forces are at work, enabling the therapist to see around the corners of a person's mind, as though looking through a psychic periscope. It is just as likely, however, that the harmony between image and emergent fact is a joint endeavor between therapist and patient. The metaphor must be sensitively responsive to actual qualities of the patient that can be observed. The mustachioed man with the prison stripes actually looked as I described him. The turbaned innocent actually emanated his contradictions. Once this poetic faithfulness is accomplished, the generality of the metaphor gives the patient the opportunity to pick those of his life's experiences which resonate with the metaphor. The therapist is thus not predicting the person's life, as a clairvoyant might, but giving the patient the framework within which to harmonize a life story with the perceptions of the therapist.

Guiding images may have momentary visibility or may make their appearance over and over. A grim visage, for example, may be only temporary, pointing to the story of some recent happening, like an argument with a friend—or it may be a theme around which most of a life revolves. In either case, the task for the guiding image is to organize those experiences seeking release with no evident vehicle through which to surface. The guiding image represents a mini-theory about the person's life, one to be tested and modified as the story of that life evolves. The thematic light which this metaphor emits helps to reduce the chaos of unbounded experience. Chaos represents a supreme innocence; it wipes out all perspective. There is much to admire in such innocence, yet in healthy function all experience arranges itself around classifications which tie experiences together and illuminate our paths.

Unfortunately, there are many abuses of such classifications. Clarifying though they may be, there is an understandable longing to take each event on its own merits. Common pigeonholing errors are evident in racial metaphors, which treat all members alike;

rigid organizational structures, which ignore individual skills of workers; stalemated negotiations, where each party sticks to his guns; and diagnostic categories, which lump symptoms together. Clearly, if one is driven by any particular guiding image and ignores what doesn't harmonize with that image, one will end up with distortion. Nevertheless, errors notwithstanding, themes will naturally become evident in any sequence of events; sensitively used, they will increase the fertility of story line. But, inevitably, the themes will change.

STORIES BEGET STORIES

Underlying all the evocative factors in the development of story line is a belief in the value of stories. Many people don't come equipped with this belief, but when they find the welcome mat is out their stories come. This hospitality doesn't have to be verbalized; it is often best communicated by the simple fact of telling stories. One will lead to another, like eating peanuts. Once, for example, when I was giving a demonstration therapy session in front of a large audience, a woman, Jan, volunteered to work with me. When I asked her what she would like out of the session, she said she would like me *to get to know her.* In wondering what she might like me to know about her, I flashed into a story about one of my elementary school teachers. She was beautiful and I loved her, but she could not have known much of my existence because I was so shy that I said virtually not a word in class. When I left class, though, I was wholly vigorous, playing on the playground or the streets or at home as though I had no limits in the world. Occasionally I would wistfully think what a gladness I would feel if my teacher could know me then, in those settings. But, of course, she never did.

Jan said that made her feel really sad because that was part of her story also, that she was, as she put it, "real, real shy." The coincidence between her experiences in school and mine is not uncommon. Confidence in commonality often serves as encouragement, even inspiration, for telling those experiences which might otherwise be thought irrelevant. Mine just hit the mark, sparking Jan to tell hers, starting from the same theme as mine but with details far different from any in my life. She went on to say that even her kindergarten record said she was terribly shy and it was still being put on her record when she graduated from high school. "So I spent 15 years being shy."

For reasons not clearly evident, talking about her shyness reminded Jan of a farm where her adoptive grandparents had lived. She felt sad thinking about them. By this time they were dead and the farm had been sold. Her grandfather had been a Danish immigrant who used to walk with his hands behind his back, Jan tagging along. Although he was a fine man, the women around him chastized him for never doing anything right. For one thing he didn't make enough money; for another he snored so loudly everyone had to go to sleep before he did. He had marvelous hands, though, and Jan could remember his touching her warmly and her own deep feelings when he died and how the neighbor boy cried.

Then, while telling her story, she was moved to call out to him that he was the only grandfather she knew and that she regretted never telling him how she loved his touching her. At this point, she felt a strong connection with him. This was so important in its own right that it didn't matter to her anymore whether I knew her or not. In a sense that was a good resolution, feeling her connection so clearly that her implied yearning to be known was replaced by a confidence in relationship. Yet, something was still missing. She seemed comfortable but reserved and this didn't fit the strong emotions she was describing. So I asked her to permit herself a greater extravagance. Otherwise, she might just abandon the story rather than finish it. When I suggested an extravagance, she realized she wanted to sing but felt too shy to do it. After only a mild nudge, she said she wanted to sing an Appalachian folk song, "I Wonder as I Wander." She wanted to sing it to me the way she had often sung it to her children. She proceeded to do it with spellbinding melodiousness and warmth—a special gift to me, to all of us present, and, by implication, to the grandfather she had never told of her love. For a painfully shy person to sing her song in front of people was a testament to her adult courage and fundamental self-respect. My story about my shyness had created a healthy contagion, a fertile source of storytelling.

The same contagion exists in group therapy, where the story of one patient will jog stories brewing within others. A community of concern grows around knowing the events in each others' lives, tapping into a richness which might ordinarily be disregarded. One man, Franklin, was disturbed because he believed his compassion for another group member's story was so strong that it was incongruous. He didn't know the people in her story so why should he be affected so strongly! Incongruity became his motif. It shadowed him everywhere, and he finally began to tell about his major incongruity. He, white, was the father of a black son.

His wife had told him on their honeymoon that she was pregnant. He might be the father or it might be a black man with whom she had slept. He was stunned and frightened, but he stayed with her. When the child arrived, he was black. When no adoption could be arranged, Franklin and his wife kept the boy and later, when he and his wife divorced, he continued to participate in raising the boy. Franklin adores the boy, now 16, and cried his heart out while telling about the beauty of his black son. In his eyes, the boy is a dream of strength and serenity. While telling his story, Franklin's sense of incongruity disappeared. What he thought of as incongruous was only what he was afraid was more than he could bear. He could bear a lot, however, and seemingly fragmented pieces of his life fit together very well.

Franklin's story and all the others in this chapter have one special function in common. They help to elaborate the sketchy impressions these people live by. Each abstraction — be it incongruity, greatness, shyness, rape, or any other quick summation of experience — serves as an introduction to detailed experience. Each kindles the therapist's curiosity. Once this curiosity is felt by patients, they, in a sense, become teachers, teaching the therapist what they are like. Seeing this knowledge reflected by the therapist in words, gestures and attentiveness, the patient may come that much closer to knowing his own truth about himself.

All these stories were just short of consciousness. None of them came from exotically deep conjecture. Simple questions, simple accenting of certain words, simple prior stories, and simple provocations were all it took to loosen the stories. Yet, in each case the telling of the story cleared the air for the teller and reduced the level of anxiety.

Of course, single stories will not usually fill out their implied story possibilities. Franklin's troublesome confusion about incongruity, for example, was recognized and relieved through telling about his black son. But to do full justice to his concerns about incongruity he may have to tell stories connected with other experiences. Perhaps his mother screamed at him to clean up his room while the kitchen was full of dirty dishes or perhaps she nagged him to study while she was glued to a noisy TV program or perhaps she pulled his ear when he didn't know what he had done wrong. Every abstraction is only a synopsis and a number of stories may be required to flesh out the theme.

Not only are the therapist and the novelist alert for the story line, but *any* person may be as well. All conversations contain interesting story lines; we may either tell our own or draw stories out from others. This may seem contrived, but it is actually the most natural thing to do. Children do it all the time, telling stories or asking others for theirs. At a conclave of storytelling, reported by Dirk Johnson in the *New York Times*, a children's librarian, Linda Neal Boyce, said that stories "tell us where we've been and where we're going. They tell us who we are." Alex Haley at the same meeting said, "When an old person dies, it's like a library has burned down." To tap this rich supply, any person may simply exercise natural curiosity, wanting to know more about any theme. This, along with thirsty listening, will lubricate the storytelling propensities of all but the most reluctant among us.

FIVE

Rhythms in Meaning

The novels of Conrad, of Hardy, of Gide, of
Camus . . . provide man with guides for the internal
search.

— Jerome S. Bruner

THE GREAT MYSTERIES within the simplest experiences were
highlighted by Freud in his raid on the psychological underground
of life. He pinpointed the unglimpsed significance of ordinary
events, normally taken only at face value. Since then events have
never had the same innocence.

For psychotherapists, the psychoanalytic keys to hidden meaning provide an expanded world of therapeutic opportunity, and, in
fact, most psychotherapists, whether Freudian or not, have become new-age detectives. In working with their patients, they
need not be immobilized by the apparent senselessness of self-
defeating behavior. Equipped with methods for decoding behavior
they have come to understand more of what they are facing. The
exhilaration of seeing new dimensions of life is intoxicating—no
less so for patients than for their psychotherapists. They both
spread the word, seeding the society with the realization that a
rose may not be a rose may not be a rose after all.

Unfortunately, when that rose is no longer seen as a rose, the experiencing mind may be bypassed. Witness the attempt to assassinate President Reagan by a young man who said he only wanted to show off for a movie star. Showing off, of course, is no crime. It is even sentimentally understandable that he would want to. On the premise that he must be crazy to exercise his sentimentality so drastically, this assassin was found innocent by a jury, although he maimed at least one person and wounded others, including the President of the United States. Clearly, in this case, the manifest event, shooting people, was moderated by its meaning, that he was crazy to be showing off that way.

The struggle between event and meaning has become recognized as a daily dynamic in everybody's life. People who tell a joke a minute are said to be starving for love and applause; mothers who require tidy bedrooms are replaying their own toilet training; competitive businessmen are trying to unseat their fathers; surgeons are expressing hidden sadism; and altruists are achieving a feeling of superiority or assuaging guilt. The population in general and psychotherapists and artists in particular are mightily tempted to look behind *everything*—and quickly. They are beguiled into believing that the depths undergirding any event are accessible.

Consider the effects of our tendency to psychoanalyze ordinary experience. One patient of mine reported an unpleasant conversation among friends. She had told them that, though she had lived in San Diego for some years, she still missed the East Coast where she grew up. This was a simple enough statement and one which could easily lead to further elaboration of her experiences in both places. One man, though, started immediately to translate the *meaning*, with little curiosity about the unfolding story. He knew she was living in the same house her husband had lived in with his now-dead previous wife, and he told my patient that she was *really* unhappy because she was martyring herself by living in a house of ghosts. Since she was still living in this house, there were, of course, ghostly elements present. But she was stunned by this self-assured interpreter, who cavalierly dismissed her *actual* experience in favor of what he *thought it meant*.

Quite irrespective of the rightness or wrongness of his assumption about this woman, what was lost to this man was the actual differences my patient perceived between East and West — what pleased her, for example, in growing up in the East and what she now missed. What was also passed over was her conscious choice to stay in the house temporarily because of the financial advantages and because her 16-year-old stepson *needed* the stability and continuity of that house. These elements of practicality and compassion have their own rightful contribution, regardless of the wisdom of the woman's decision to stay in the house or whether she also sought martyrdom. If manifest practicality and compassion are dismissed in favor of this woman's supposedly *real* purpose — martyrdom — innocent perception takes a back seat. When this happens commonly, as it does in psychological circles, we have the basis for maddening confusion. How are we to distinguish between what "really" is and what only *seems* to be?

Free Expression

Psychoanalysis has contributed one of the most liberating expressive instruments of all time, and that is the concept of free association. Freed from the grammatical, purposeful, moral, and logical requirements of ordinary communication, the individual can string out thoughts which are, at best, ambiguously connected. They might seem quite psychotic. But the "psychosis" of the person free associating is only temporary; a slight flick of the mind returns that person to recognizable syntax.

The now familiar realization which occurred to those early psychoanalysts and their freely associating patients is that, through this peculiar connection of thoughts, certain symbolic referents are commonly revealed. Misty though these allusions might be, they are used to conjure up an oasis of enlightenment to those thirsting for deep meaning. These temptations for fresh insight grew because of the inspiring discoveries of many patients. In the worst scenarios, however, hardly anything seems too obscure to be understood. Even the dimmest connections are often transformed by translation into ordained meanings.

In the age of the psychological detective it has been taken for granted that, though undeciphered, certain meanings already exist for each person's behavior. One need only find them by following clues, Sherlock Holmes style. A word here about loving daffodils with their cup-like form and a word there about hating trains when they go through tunnels and we have the oedipal implications which account for a young man's impotence. This approach, putting two and two together to find the answer to the psychological puzzle, can be cognitively exciting and often leads to necessary illuminations. However, it only takes account of the symbolic relationship of the present event to an obscured part of the past—half of the potential. The other half, an alternative to this detective approach, is to follow the symbolic present as it moves forward into the future. As stories unfold, meanings are not yet formed as present events impel people into new behaviors. The new happenings and the evolving meanings are not just old ones newly uncovered; they have never previously existed. It is like the difference between lifting a cloth that has been covering an already baked pie and baking a pie from scratch.

Here is a therapeutic example of the symbol's two options—to move backward in giving meaning to an event by revealing the already formed past or to move forward into the unconstructed future. Suppose that laughing with one's therapist symbolizes permission to play as a child in an adult world. In pointing backward, this symbol may refer to past childish behavior, permissible until five years of age and forbidden thereafter. Insights into the forbidden, as well as remembering and accepting the earlier freedom, have opened the patient to this laughter. Or, taking the other option, the laughter, once aroused, may point forward without reference to what has already happened, symbolizing those many opportunities for laughter that are to come. Similarly, without any attention to old events, there are many other occasions when, say, a young woman can discover, following a series of new actions, that her father welcomes her as never before; that unfamiliar sexual practices are not evil, as she may have thought; or that leadership is no longer beyond her. Plainly, though meanings are available and helpful to everyone, they may come from the unknown givens of the past or the inspirations of continuing experience, an abstraction of new possibilities. Or, on many other occasions, meaning may not matter at all.

This versatility in the management of meanings has been the subject of extensive exploration, not only among psychotherapists but also among artists, who have contributed greatly to the loosening of familiar connections between events and meanings. Alert to expressive freedom, they have, in explorations parallel to free association, found their own confirmation of the plasticity of mind. The plasticity they have found—as represented by Dali's limp watches, Picasso's manipulation of shadows as if they were solid forms, Beckett's characters who wait in limbo, and Joyce's idiosyncratic syntax—have given new latitude to the perceivers of these most elemental experiences. Comparably, relativity theory has added its transcendence of the given reality, showing truth to depend on the individual's own position. Taking all these outlooks into account, it is clear that the meanings of any event, depending as they do upon the perspective of the observer, are not to be pinned down like a specimen butterfly. Since nothing is only as it seems to be, all the many other things it may also be are new themes to play with.

Although Freud, by infusing even paltry events with meaning, increased our interest in the rhythms between event and meaning, the artists of our age are by no means as driven to probe for clear meaning. Many of them have taken another road, seeking a release from meanings. For some artists, at the end of the nineteenth century and into the twentieth, form came first and the subject, or meaning, second. Whistler, for example, gave priority to form by calling his portrait of his mother "Arrangement in Grey and Black." But you could still recognize his mother.

In the new art forms meanings are often unrecognizable. Sometimes, particularly in recent years, this obscurity has even become chic, partly because of the artist's intention to abolish familiar meanings and partly because of the gullibility of people trying to keep up-to-date by pretending not to care about meaning. There are some who claim that the artist is only concerned with pure expression; that is, meaningful communication to anyone else is only incidental. Others, who do want to affect others, want to do so by registering raw experience in their work. They hope that sadness, exhilaration, horror, disgust, devotion, emptiness, etc., can all be felt in their essence, without the neutralizing intrusion of meaning. This is an attempt to restore experience itself to ascendancy in an otherwise overly rationalistic world. It is hoped that the event, unmediated by the distraction imposed by meaning, will take on a new freshness, a unique identity, seen for itself, not for the class of events to which it could be said to belong.

The yearning among artists for innocent, uncategorized experience is only partly satisfied, matched as it is against the human reflex to give meaning to events. When artists bypass meaning, many people are prompted to search for meaning anyway. Instead of concentrating on these events as events, as the artist may intend, people instead conjecture about meaning. When they fail to get even glimmerings of intended meanings or to derive some special personal meaning, they are often frustrated and the event itself becomes easily dismissible.

In the struggle between conventional standards and the radical twentieth century attempt either to obscure meaning or exclude it, one conclusion seems evident: *There is no given proportion in personal experience between an event and its meaning.* You may be more interested in the meanings of any event, while another person cares primarily about the event itself. Where these proportions go haywire, the individual will run into trouble. Sooner or later, the disproportionate concern with either meaning or event is going to exclude vital considerations. People who heavily emphasize events and relegate meaning to insignificance may live a life that is largely impulsive, ephemeral, purposeless, or disjointed. Their lives may be like Shakespeare's "tale told by an idiot, all sound and fury, signifying nothing." If, on the other hand, no event is taken simply as it occurs but is always scrutinized for its profounder meaning, you have a life of omens and forebodings, of seeing the event only as a portent, never living it for its own vibrant sake.

INTERPLAY OF MEANING AND EVENTS

Two classic novels, Melville's *Moby Dick* and Kafka's *The Castle*, represent a different management of this interplay of meaning with events. *Moby Dick* can be read innocently for the face value of its events. Giving the novel its greatness, however, is the larger illumination it produces for the life of the reader and for understanding humanity. For the reader not interested in such implications, it is nevertheless an interesting story about a ship's captain obsessed with a particular whale. What makes the hunt especially interesting is that this whale is renowned. He is also personalized by the captain, who was previously injured by the whale. Interest is further tapped by the inclusion of danger, revenge, indomitability, the mysteries of the sea, the primitivism of animals, and the requirement for coordination among the men. Though the allegorical implications add an unconscious stake in the events, there need be no awareness of these implications. The burden of the story is carried by such simple issues as: Will the whale be caught? Will the people survive? How skillful will they be in the hunt? Do they trust each other? Do the readers like them or not? Do they cheer for the whale or the ship's captain?

Kafka's writing is quite different. Readers are often required to suspend their interest in the narrative if they want to integrate elements which don't readily fit together. Easy surface connections of events are not available. Readers must make their own sense of strange allusions, distortions of time, inexplicable motivations and even a misty geography. When reading *The Castle*, they must set aside the need for familiar sequences and attend as to a dream. The surrealistic flashes, like the elements of a dream, leave as much unsaid as said. Like the dream, the compelling events, left in disarray, beg for completion. For many readers this comes with a search for the meaning implicit in the events, as the events themselves recede in clarity.

K, though he is the main character, is himself a wispy figure. He is a surveyor mysteriously called to work for the castle. The reader doesn't know where he comes from, what he looks like, or even who hired him. He comes to report for his work with only the most ghostly information about what is required or how he would go about doing it. Plainly no ordinary surveyor would take a job under such obscure circumstances, yet there is no fleshing out of this apparition-like existence.

But the reader tries anyway to fill the gaps in comprehensibility, pulled forward by the masterful writing and by the oddly attractive strangeness of the events. Certain elements of story line, though not in clear sequence, are interesting in their own right, so the reader is able to transcend the exclusions of meaning and supply them. The reader may ask whether we all live similarly, from day-to-day, not knowing where we came from or where we are going.

The events in K's life are dwarfed by the more philosophical intimations that all people live meaningless and depersonalized lives. The revelation reminds people of their own lives, but what makes *The Castle* a classic work is that it also reveals the state of society at large.

Valuable as this message may be from the point of view of social awareness, the diminished importance of the novel's actual events becomes a source of distortion. Awareness of the struggle against depersonalization or meaninglessness does not alter the fact that much in our lives is very personal and much of it has very clear meaning. Consider, for example, the following event. Your son is inexplicably late; after hours of sleepless anxiety you finally hear his car pull into the driveway. That is a very personal experience. Now able to go to sleep, you are relieved—he is alive and you will be able to continue to do many of the things you love to do with him. It is a very simple event that requires no profound symbolic transformation.

Of course, other factors may influence your simple reactions. Are you anxious about your own unconscious sexual fantasies and, therefore, wondering what your son is doing out so late? Are you replaying the death of a loved relative? Are you insecure about your own life and wanting to live it out through your son? Are you guilty about how badly you have sometimes treated him?

Selectively these questions may be well worth answering. In some circles, particularly the psychoanalytic, such prospects for meaning are habitually tapped. However, when this search is overplayed, the nourishment naturally available in simple experience is dissipated. For instance, in one group of psychoanalytically oriented psychiatric residents, not yet seasoned and therefore vulnerable to stereotypical searches for meaning, the group members could hardly hear a word uttered without wondering *why* he or she said it. At the other pole of naivete, we find two characters in the movie "Diner" talking about an Ingmar Bergman movie. One says, "What's the movie about?" The other answers, "It's symbolic." The first one asks, "Who's that guy up there?" The other answers, "It's Death, walking on the beach." The first one observes, "I've been to Atlantic City a hundred times and I *never* saw Death walking on the beach."

SCRAMBLING THE MIND

There are times, as in Kafka's work, when it is advisable to separate meaning from its familiar supports in order, paradoxically, to get a point across. The dadaists, who also wanted to destructure familiar reality, were interested in the shock value of their loose associations. Trying to undo the rigidity of mind which had tethered people to destructive values and behavior, they were reacting especially against the irrationality of war. They saw the killing and maiming of millions as a manifestation of irrationality and in effect said, "If you want irrationality, we'll give you irrationality — where it is not hypocritically masked." By erasing rationality, they intended to return our minds to a state of tabula rasa, described long ago by John Locke. In attempting to dissemble the mind, they would free it for new learning. Old meanings obstructed the opportunities for change, and they opted to throw out what they perceived as prohibitively prearranged mental connections. In both the dada and surrealist movements, the need to create change led to scrambling the mind's familiar, linear process.

The reorganization of experience, relieved of linear constriction, requires a freedom to shuttle back and forth between any intended line of development and a free associative unruliness. The mind may best remain open to the nonlinear experience when the individual is confident that the detouring ideas, interesting in themselves, will make sense sooner or later. Sometimes this faith will come from intimations that the divergent thoughts will pay off, and sometimes it will come from sheer trust in the artistry of the guide.

A good example of this trust may be found in the work of hypnotherapist Milton Erickson, who often told parable-like stories to his patients. For significant intervals the stories might not make sense to the listener. Erickson's patient or trainee, aware of his ingenious sense of secret appropriateness, was willing to stay with his seemingly unrelated stories with their more or less hidden messages until their implicit instruction was revealed. Sometimes the revelation would come right away, sometimes it would come later, and sometimes effects would come unconsciously without any revelation at all.

Sidney Rosen, in *My Voice Will Go with You,* tells the story of Kathleen, a student in one of Erickson's training seminars who was phobic about vomiting. Erickson talked to her of many things: at first, of Arctic Ocean walruses, penguins, whales, scuba divers and plankton. Then he went on to tell about woodpeckers and about a birdwatcher who ingeniously emptied out the throat of the woodpecker. Finally, he described certain regurgitative functions of the woodpeckers. By the time he was done with his story he had painted a vivid picture of natural function among these creatures. Erickson and Kathleen then went on to other topics in a rather desultory way, with only scant attention to Kathleen's vomiting. In the end Erickson did make some humorous allusions to vomiting. The rest was up to her, armed as she was with an implanted appreciation of the function of vomiting within a world of natural variety.

Of course, the position of the dadaists and surrealists, as well as the cubists, is drastic compared to this example of Erickson's indirect relevance. In the cubist method, an entire image is broken down into its parts. To see the strangely arranged parts as a recognizable whole requires increased attention. One may, for example, see arms and legs, here or there, but not be able to reconstruct the person from these parts, except as an extrapolation in the perceiver's mind.

For those willing to accept the challenge of the cubists, the perception and reconstruction of strangely placed parts taps into a large energy reservoir, calling for a new level of creative participation. Although this is a challenge to one's perceptual creativity, it is a fairly safe one, because even if the parts never come back together, little is lost. At the very least the viewer may find that clear identity is a less rigid necessity than might otherwise have been supposed.

In everyday life and in psychotherapy, where flexibility about identity is also a necessary goal, the personal stakes are higher. When people are faced with aspects of personality which they feel do not harmonize with their own sense of identity, anxiety may be high. When, for example, a person explores his or her own peculiar fantasies or oddly angled face or experiences sexual arousal when washing an infant's genitals or excitement about the death of a friend or a new feeling that can't quite be grasped, that person needs confidence that self-identity continues as a unified whole. For the viewer of the cubist or surrealistic painting, seeing the whole does not always happen (nor does it need to). However, in "real" life the person feels that it must.

Mystery vs. Confusion

A simple therapeutic vignette will show how a minimum of emphasis on understanding some poorly understood connections between events evolved into a meaningful unit of experience. One day Oscar, a graduate student in my therapy course, asked me before class whether I was all right. He thought I looked depressed. I was pleased he was willing to ask and thanked him for caring, but said I didn't want to talk about it. Then I forgot the conversation.

Just before our next class meeting, Oscar came up again. This time he told me he had almost gone crazy the past week. Would I mind if during the class meeting he just got up if he needed to and walked around? I said of course I wouldn't mind. I didn't know whether his trouble was any of my business, any more than he knew whether my trouble was any of his the week before. I was interested, though, and he went on to tell me he had been to a hospital emergency room. He apparently had had a severe anxiety attack. Still a little wobbly, he sounded as though his mind had temporarily skipped the track and some people at the hospital had helped him to get it back on. The track was still slippery, though.

Listening to Oscar I remembered how once, while lying on a couch, I meditated myself onto its edge, as though it were a cliff. In a trance-like emergency, I teetered there precariously, then chose to let go of this "cliff-hanger." As I let go I fell, in meditative delusion, as though into an abyss, but when I landed I had made only the short fall to the floor.

I flashed then to other falls. At five, I had gone to a movie theater with the boys on the street where my family had recently moved. We sat in the first row. Between me and the screen there was a space, an extremely dark space. The movie was Lon Chaney's "Unholy Three," an old thriller. Accidentally, I dropped my cap into the space and, at five, I only knew that it had fallen irretrievably into darkness. The vastness into which my cap — and, by implication, my small body — could drop scared me. I recognized a primordial danger while conjuring up my cap's presumable entry into eternity. Now I know that the space was only an orchestra pit.

These surrealistic flashes warmed my mind to Oscar's experience. We talked some more and it was time for class to begin; class time was to be spent in a demonstration group-therapy experience rather than a lecture. At first people were slow to speak. Then, perhaps spurred by our conversation, perhaps sucked in by the silence, Oscar told the class about his panic. After a half-hour of sympathetic exchange with other group members, he suddenly decided he wanted to go out for a walk. Was he sure that was what he wanted, I asked. Oscar said yes. When I asked if he would be back soon, he said yes. He looked as though he knew what he wanted, and left.

He was still on everyone's mind. They *knew* he wanted to be on his own, and he *knew* he could come back whenever he wanted to. Nevertheless, there was a curious dread, beyond likelihood, that he might disregard our availability. After some further wheel-spinning about whether or not we should invite him back in, one person quietly got up, went out, and came sauntering back with Oscar. He had been gone about 15 minutes and was ready to be back, even glad to be invited back. He told us he had left because the woman next to him had touched him tenderly while he had been talking and this had frightened him. He could not allow the strong feeling her touch evoked. Though he knew how warmly he felt, the feeling became detached. Then, worse, this split seemed to him mad. As he talked about it, the split diminished; instead, he soon began to feel "all together," his warm feeling reinstated. By then the feeling was simply tender and he lost his self-consciousness about it.

In this example there are several events which set the story's course. Each of them had implicit meaning but only once was the meaning verbally articulated. The series of events started with my student's asking whether I was depressed. The reason why he asked was unclear and whether I was depressed or not was never clarified. It was also uncertain whether a bond formed between us concerning psychological suffering. The next event simply happened without our knowing much about the meaning of the first. That is, he came to me and offered the unsolicited information about his panic state and requested freedom to walk around. Both Oscar's and my feelings were considerably stronger this time than the first and I did some metaphorical meandering about primordial danger. This gave some thematic structure to Oscar's experience.

Next Oscar told his classmates about his anxiety state—and he left. His leaving was received as a dangerous event. Then came the rescue. Only during the next event did we receive the gift of meaning, when Oscar told us why he left—the unbearable sense of intimacy with the woman next to him. Here we saw a hint of connections between his hot feelings and the dangers of his mind being split in two. Then safety at last. The mystery seemed momentarily resolved as the vignette ended happily. The remaining mystery was for the future. Only as an appendix, with little detail, can it be said that he seemed in good spirits for the rest of the semester's classes, requiring no special focus and making pertinent remarks related to classroom themes.

The mystery inherent to an interest in Oscar's life calls forth a number of questions. What do these events say about his life, or life generally? Does it have meaning for the reader or the psychotherapist? Does this story tell anything about sexual boundaries, about tenderness, about freedom of expression, about people caring to hear each other out, about the resiliency in certain varieties of madness? What about Oscar's parents, his feelings of shame, his robust recovery? Each event spawns its own connectedness with innumerable other events. On and on, meanings tempt the exploratory mind.

At times, however, the therapist must set aside pursuit of these mysteries for the sake of immediately clarifying experience. Lives may be at stake. Or psychologically dangerous decisions, such as divorce, marriage, having a child, changing jobs, or generally rocking the boat, may make the leisure of mystery hard to sustain. Where uncertainty requires a premature clarification, the pressure for immediate decision or action can result in confusion. Oscar was more of a mystery to me, however, than a source of confusion, perhaps because he did not seem to be in immediate emergency and had other continuing therapeutic attention. Where pressure for immediate clarity can be reduced, as it often can, the mystery can unfold its special clarity in its own rightful time.

In order to get over the confusion which urgency creates, people will often generalize about events, so that quick meanings will be readily available. All the "isms" help to do this. Sexism, for one, makes it easy to think one knows people of both sexes without experiencing them individually. If women are thought to be sentimental, it will take innumerable experiences of their cool, rational decision-making to overcome this belief. If men are thought to be brusque and unfeeling, it will take a lot of compassion before their unexpected sensitivity will be recognized. Quick conclusions negate both mystery and confusion by providing premature meaning and obscuring underlying possibilities. Here are some examples of quick translations which portend more than they should: Mother wouldn't approve of Jack, so conversations with him don't matter. A young man's life begins at 16 because that's when he suddenly starts to shoot up in height. A brilliant day at work is not worth much because there is no spouse to come home to. An insult causes despair because it means nobody appreciates you. If you get tired it means you're weak, and if you make a mistake you're incompetent. In each case, the quick meaning overshadows the real range of what is actually possible. It negates events which may not fit the conclusions and reduces freedom to move in unpredictable directions, leaving stumps of unrealized potentiality.

EXPLANATIONS

The move to quick conclusions, common also among psychotherapists, has led to widespread disillusion about the therapeutic effect of explanations. Many therapists nowadays prefer to let events speak for themselves but, alas, understanding does not always come spontaneously. Without explanations therapeutic understanding may never come to some people. The same is true in the arts. Looking to music, we see that it comes as close as the arts do to raw experience, easily received without concern for its meaning. But even here, Jonathan Saville, a music and theater critic, has offered a plea for *understanding* it. In reviewing Webern's "Six Bagatelles," he writes about his own experience of learning to appreciate Webern. He played him over and over; through the innumerable repetitions of the music he discovered that Webern's bagatelles are "concentrated dramas, pared down to fundamentals: an initial state of being, an action, a conflict, a climax, a denouement — all within the space of thirty seconds." He then goes on to say:

> What makes this music so strange, so apparently incomprehensible, is its compression in time. "I was walking slowly along the road made of a sort of rubber," relates the dreamer, "and then the road tilted, and my father was falling toward me dressed in a black suit without any buttons." After hours of consultation with the dreamer's psychoanalyst, it emerges that this tiny dream, so quick in the telling, has compressed the needs, fears, furies, and dilemmas of a lifetime, along with a myriad of persons, places, and events. The emotions are intense, but disguised; the events manifold, but fused into one or two; the breadth is ruthlessly circumscribed, the depth is infinite. That is what Anton von Webern's music is like . . . the pretense ought to be abandoned that the audience can appreciate or learn to appreciate Webern on their own. . . . They can't. With the ordinary kind of exposure in public concerts, it will not be fifty years but *never* that everyone will experience this music as their natural kind of music . . . someone ought to explain the music to the audience, illustrating the explanation with concrete examples played by the musicians.

Given the complexity of experience which Saville has described, it is respectful of the human mind for us to recognize that the simple reflex to understanding must be augmented by the special clarity which explanations may contribute. The complaint against explanation should be directed against the mistaken belief that explanations are enough or against the poor quality of many explanations — not against well-timed, illuminating ones. Perhaps it will be argued that explanation is just warmed-over psychoanalytic interpretation. Indeed, it is. The realization that insight is central to psychological change is one of Freud's major contributions, opening an entire century to the mysteries of the unconscious.

For example, Dominic, a patient of mine, hadn't paid me for over a year and through secretarial error I had not known about it. He didn't have the money but had never said so. When I discovered this, I told him he was behaving like his Mafia cousins, whom he had presumably cut out of his mind. He was stunned by my observation because he had been very disdainful of them. But he was excited. From his depressed and futile attitude about life— which was his common state—he was jarred into seeing the adventure of robbing me right under my nose. A continuing revitalization in his life dates back to that moment of insight when he was able to understand his unwillingness to do what other people are supposed to do. This understanding released the *energy* of the gangster, replacing the *guilt* he had been chronically suffering.

The power of explanation in psychotherapy is corrupted by two errors. One is to isolate explanations from behavior, thereby giving the explanations a position of distance from the events being explained. For example, Dominic's Mafia background had livelier meaning to him in the context of his robbing me than as an abstract truth. The second error is to use explanations too often. They crowd people's minds and obscure the uniqueness of the explained event. About such excesses, John Updike, in an interview with George Plimpton, has said, "Narratives should not be *primarily* packages for psychological insights, though they should contain them, like raisins in buns."

What Dominic experienced in this session also harmonizes with Maxwell Anderson's rule for a successful play, as related by Josh Logan. Anderson said, "A play should take its protagonist through a series of experiences which lead to a climactic moment toward the end when he *learns* something, *discovers* something about himself that he could have known all along but has been blind to. . . . The audience must feel and see the leading man become wiser. . . ." That's what happened to Dominic. He learned a special truth about his gangster background and by this knowledge was able to reexperience both energy and enterprise, each giving greater dimension to his background than the lawlessness which had filled his mind.

These moments of special recognition, the times when the mind expands to give new meaning to experiences, are the signposts of connection between any single event and the larger ground of life. But meanings are not limited to these moments. They are all over the place, whether they stand out as guides or unnoticeably insinuate themselves. It makes a difference whether I interpret your remark as snide or as an affectionate tease, whether I take your praise as genuine or a motivational trick, whether I see myself as greedy or simply of hearty appetite. These choices in meaning, when they become wrongly skewed, are tenacious, given up only reluctantly. And the profusion of errors in meaning eventually engages the attention of writers and psychotherapists. They will never run out of material as they seek to turn old meanings around or add new meanings that have been overlooked.

SIX

Internal Dialogue

And out of what one sees and hears and out
Of what one feels, who could have thought to make
So many selves, so many sensuous worlds
As if the air, the mid-day air, was swarming . . .
— Wallace Stevens, *Esthetique du Mal*

I ONCE HAD A MOTTLED CAT, black, white, and tawny. When she had three kittens, one was black, another white and the third tawny, each one a pure rendition of the parts of their conglomerate mother. People are speckled also, losing their purity through the mutual influence of all their many characteristics. But the composite person, just like my cat, retains the potential purity of each characteristic. Although an ambitious person, for example, loses the purity of his ambitiousness when he is also lazy, this loss is not permanent. When characteristics become fuzzy or when they are crowded out altogether by repression, writers and therapists must have the vision to see past these beclouding effects, to clarify those constituents of the person that have been moderated or muzzled. Carl Sandburg, for one, cuts through when he writes in one of his poems about the wolf in himself — the hog also, and the baboon. Then he goes on to say:

O, I got a zoo, I got a menagerie, inside my ribs, under my bony head, under my red-valve heart—and I got something else: it is a man-child heart, a woman-child heart: it is a father and mother and lover: it came from God Knows Where: it is going to God-Knows-Where—For I am the keeper of the Zoo: I say yes and no: I sing and kill and work: I am a pal of the world: I came from the wilderness.

With all these characters living inside the person, the therapist working with any individual is actually doing group therapy. Through speech and behavior each part of the person gives clues to its existence. The therapist must guide the individual in identifying these parts, letting them speak clearly for themselves, and finding a place for each part in the community of the self. To feel whole in the face of great internal diversity is a major challenge in the life of any person. On the other hand, inaccessibility of certain parts for inclusion into the whole is a potential source of disturbance.

The splitting of the person into parts is most often represented by polarization into opposite characteristics such as cruelty and kindness, boldness and timidity, or grandiosity and humility. It is also true, however, that the internal struggle is populated by more subtle qualities, all of which contribute to the total behavior. These multilarities, representing the many sides of the individual, are present in clusters of potential experience rather than only in polarities. A peace advocate, for example, might be troubled not only by his polar anger—against an opponent of his views—but also by his need to spend more time at work, by his distaste for many of his associates in the peace movement, by his cynicism, by the frustrations of failure, or even by people commenting on the mole on his upper lip. These elements of his many-sidedness may be as disharmonious with work in the peace movement as the simple polar opposite.

In either case, whether looking at polarities or multilarities, the therapist's expectation is that those parts which are disharmonious have poor contact with each other and exist only as more or less segregated elements. The restitution of internal harmony comes from the renewal of good communication among the parts. This is accomplished by personifying each part and giving it a voice. As each part speaks in dialogue with the other and as the communication is improved, the contact between the parts becomes sharper and they begin to experience each other in a new light.

For example, a woman named Caroline was tortured by her indecision about having a baby. Her suffering was growing greater with each tick of the biological clock. Plainly, there were at least two sides of her — one wanting a child, the other opposed. The two sides, personified, each had stereotyped attitudes about themselves and about the other side. I asked Caroline to play out a dialogue between these parts. At the start their positions were so fixed that a fresh dialogue seemed unlikely. The one who did not want the child was the manifestly dominant one, although not so dominant that she had won out. In spite of not having been able to settle the issue, she was certain she was right and she could eloquently spell out exactly why she didn't want a baby. She knew her life was going well and she didn't want it disrupted by the needs of a child. She was also convinced that at the age of 35 she ran great risks in getting pregnant, and that, since her brother had congenital heart trouble, she was in danger of having a defective baby. She also knew that her husband would leave her with all the responsibilities. And she was sure this was no world in which to raise a child.

At no time in her opening statements did this side take any account of the needs of the other, whom she saw only as weak. She could get away with it because the side that wanted a child was intimidated by the other side, could not think well in the face of the dominating onslaught, and was reduced not to crying but to dripping from her eyes — a passive, defeated shell. The supposedly superior position was maintained only by ignoring the sabotaging influence of the side who wanted a baby and who, though feeling she had little basis for argument, would not give up, whining her way to a stand-off. She would whimperingly allude to the feeling — sentimentalized — that she might be missing the special pleasures of parenthood, without which there could be no personal maturity. Although she said she wanted a baby, she got across no strong sense of personal loss. Her feelings seemed more like those of a person who believes there is a God only to be on the right side should it prove to be true. In spite of this minimal conviction, Caroline's misery was powerful enough to hamstring the opposition, who could not budge her from her holed-in intuitive position that a child was crucial to her existence.

After several exchanges in the dialogue, the side wanting the baby became more clearly aware of her futility, and then it hit her that she was not saying the things she wanted to say. She proceeded to attack, eloquently pointing out the narcissism of the part that didn't want the baby, pinpointing her cowardly and unnecessary fears, and accusing her of closing her mind to any experiences she couldn't fully control. At this point she began to get through. By the time the two sides were finished they were having a conversation worthy of equals—not a resolution yet, but a sense of one side toughening up to a position of validity and the other softening to a position of personal warmth. Then, with each side more respectful of the other, Caroline developed a curious freedom about her relationship to babies. When she saw a mother and child wrangling in a supermarket, she was relieved she did not have a baby. But this relief did not mean she *could not* have a baby. On the other side, when she visited her brother's home she played with her infant niece happily for the first time, but she realized this did not mean she *had* to have a baby.

Although her internal harmony greatly relieved her of the general pressure, she was not ready for a decision. However, following this experience, a breakthrough came on another front. Her perfectionistic attitudes had also stymied her in her job, where she had been wavering on a crucial but difficult research project. After her mind became loosened in the baby dialogue, she coincidentally took off on this project and is now practically finished. Change can be contagious; new learnings in one mental arena will commonly cross over to provide beneficial effects in others.

CONTACT

In creating a dialogue among parts of a person, the prime task is to improve the quality of the contact. The parts, alienated, will not, at first, talk straight with each other. They each know the script and, not wanting to change it, will play their roles as they have been familiarly formed. Only when a meeting of the minds has been achieved will each become something of what the other requires.

The reason the alienated parts have become masters of misconnection is that they are afraid they will be harmfully influenced by the other part. There is plenty to be afraid of. If you don't like to fight and you talk to the part of you that wants to join a gang, you are in danger; if you are deeply religious, you will shun the atheistic side of you; if you have strong sexual prohibitions, you will be frightened by the sexual side of you. The therapist, counteracting these impasses, must recognize various impediments to dialogue, such as digressions, stonewalling, failing to object when objections are called for, misunderstanding what has been said, flavorless reactions and any other sources of misconnection. Once making new connections, you may find it exciting to be aggressive, though not necessarily joining a gang. Or you may discover a broader view of religion, though not necessarily becoming an atheist. Or you may yield to sexuality without becoming wanton or vulgar. Each part in the dialogue risks taking on some aspects of the other. Whereas these parts seem incompatible in the beginning, there are actually fewer incompatibilities than one would suppose. However, that is a bet that one may either win or lose.

This struggle to maintain the purity of one's own position against the inroads of opposing forces is apparent not only on the personal level but also on societal and even international levels. China and the United States, for example, were isolated from one another for a long time, allowing only minimal communication and each fearing the influence of the other. In recent years, communication has increased, although it is still tightly controlled. The result has been increased influence in both directions. Simple examples of this influence are the growing use of acupuncture in the United States and the surge of private entrepreneurship in China.

Although the contact between the two countries has been increasing, each willing to risk its own way of life, the magnitude of danger in the minds of the most suspicious people is exemplified by Margaret Atwood in her novel, *Surfacing*. Through the voice of her heroine, a Canadian, she says about American hunters who visit Canada:

"They're what's in store for us, what we are turning into. They spread themselves like a virus, they get into the brain and take over the cells and the cells change from inside and the ones that have the disease can't tell the difference. Like the Late Show sci-fi movies, creatures from outer space, body snatchers injecting themselves into you, dispossessing your brain, their eyes blank eggshells behind the dark glasses. If you look like them and talk like them and think like them, you are them . . . "

Closer to home, we see these fears represented in the careful attention many parents give to their children's selection of friends. If the parents worry about what their children may pick up from certain contacts—drugs, diseases, or antisocial values—they will be upset and wary about these contacts. At the same time, young people's lives are broadened and enriched by contact with customs and habits different from their own. Discerning perception is required to distinguish highly dangerous threats, like drugs, from insignificant ones that may be related to snobbishness, like having friends who eat salami rather than paté.

The greatest sense of danger from the influencing part comes when there is a polarization of positions. Love and hate seem prohibitively antithetical when in their extreme forms they might call, on the one hand, for lifelong, dedicated commitment and, on the other, for murder. Reducing the burden of emotions, like loving and hating, helps to make them each acceptable. Smiling does not require undue commitment and grimacing does not lead to murder. Yet many people incorrectly read love and hate into milder feelings. Dialogue will help them to make the necessary discrimination.

SAFE OPPORTUNITIES

The broad-minded person accepts forbidden characteristics in himself, as well as in others. It is easier to do this when it is not very dangerous. Imagination enables us to safely identify with characteristics that would be forbidden in action. One can imagine being self-seeking, vulgar, dominating, or even murderous, without exercising any of these characteristics. The stakes are lower when fantasies are disconnected from "reality." To fantasize, for example, about making a 50-yard run for a touchdown is low risk when you know that you are not likely to get into a game with vicious people eager to acquaint you with your poor judgment. Yet, even though you are not a football player, your athletic, agile, courageous aspects gain recognition in the fantasy.

To safely tap into a neglected characteristic, it is helpful to create an intermediate reality where the various parts of a person can engage in dialogue. This form of practicing the forbidden prepares for the more threatening prospects in the world out there. It's no different from practicing the piano before giving a recital.

Novels provide another safe landscape for experiencing new situations and feelings at a distance. Novelists themselves are perhaps in a riskier position than their readers because in the very act of creation they become more steeped in the characters and situations than the casual reader. For those readers who take their inner life seriously, however, the distinction between the threat of the real experience and the threat of the mentally crafted experience is often blurred. Intensely absorbed, a person will experience the grandness of sensation in the crafted experience as though it were real.

A similar option is available in psychotherapy. Either the patient or the therapist makes a judgment about the depth of personal involvement required. Suppose, for example, you were to become highly identified with a risky characteristic inside yourself, such as the one represented by Mr. Hyde in Robert Louis Stevenson's famous tale, *Dr. Jekyll and Mr. Hyde.* Soon there is no doubt in your mind that somewhere inside you the specter of Mr. Hyde lurks. For most people, those who have severely isolated their unwanted characteristics from their permissible ones, the return of the forbidden might be too fearful to bear. Dr. Jekyll would prevail. Witnessing the emergence of your hidden characteristic, your readiness to experience this side helps you come as close as you can to feeling the forbidden. In safe seclusion with the therapist, you are then enabled to cross one more fear out of the mind's inventory.

PRIORITIES VIOLATED

Characteristics may be isolated for reasons other than fear. Sometimes the characteristic simply interferes with one of higher priority. One woman, Dolores, complained that the magic had gone out of her year-old marriage. Her husband had without notice taken in his 11-year-old son from a previous marriage. However, he was unwilling to enforce the discipline which both of them had agreed was necessary. Dolores, having by now reached the end of her rope, was unable to have even a civil relationship with the boy. Her relationship with her husband was in danger of going down the drain. She felt beleaguered and self-righteous. She also had an agitated sense of defeat—energetic but hopeless. Her body was as tight as her attitude.

In a series of dialogues initiated to elicit more fruitful contact with her husband and her stepson, Dolores could only repeat her grievances and call forth sterile responses. That is just what makes dialogue infertile. When I later asked her to tell me about her life as an 11-year-old, she told me about the thrills she felt while riding horses and remembered she had few responsibilities in her own household. After she warmed to this 11-year-old side of herself, I asked her to be this 11-year-old and speak to her 28-year-old self. The 11-year-old in Dolores just said two words, "Loosen up." These simple words flipped her right out of her sour perspective. She immediately loosened up her body throughout and, as though she had been let out of cage, began to laugh hilariously. For the first time in this session, one could see in her the qualities which she must have brought to the "magical" relationship she originally had with her husband. Her internal politics had closed the door on this voice because it would have prematurely undercut her policy of anger with her stepson for destroying the idyllic privacy of her life and with her husband for not supporting her more in her new parental responsibility.

The identity of alienated parts is often obscured. Dolores behaved as though she had never been 11 and as though she knew nothing about 11-year-olds. Inside, she knew very well what it was like to be 11, but she had submerged it. This is common. The veiled characteristic never raises its hand to say it is there. For example, if a person is dependent but determined not to be, the only manifestation of this dependency might be an incongruously imploring look or a subtly yearning tilt of the head. The only sign of rage might be the clipped sound of someone's words, as though he were slicing the tip of a cigar.

Another example of a person hiding an important side of himself is one young man who was hell-bent on making money, an ambition considered crass in the school milieu where he had spent the last ten years. Not feeling that he could allow himself to be money hungry, he fooled himself, as well as his wife, by telling her they needed financial security and he must go on working the long hours she was objecting to. The resulting friction between them was reaching desperate proportions because having a lot of money was not a high priority for her.

During a dialogue between the part of himself that wanted to make money and the part that resisted, the money-making part began to reveal a motive beyond security. Making money turned out to be exciting in itself. This young man wanted to outdo his father, whose success challenged him. Security was the least of his concerns. There was as much thrill for him in money-making as there would be for others in playing football. When this man played out the part of himself that *wanted to make money*, he was able to say what was true for that part, quite irrespective of any contradiction with his more customary priorities. Once he voiced this excitement, both he and his wife laughed at the absurdity of his censorship. Then they talked to each other about their wishes without having to cope with the screen of poverty.

Writers are especially tuned in to hints of internal diversity. Their imagination permits them to create extrapolations from the clues they see all around them and to raise these to a threshold of reality. John Updike, for one, in *The Centaur*, describes the experience of a teacher who, in his own classroom, has just been shot in the ankle by an arrow. This brings to mind the mythical centaur, a composition of man and horse, who, having been shot by a poisoned arrow, feels so much pain that he prays for mortality. Swiftly the reader is marshalled into this particular classroom, where the things he would ordinarily identify with are stretched beyond normal recognition. In this classroom both Updike and the reader can feel, yes, I do know what it is like to be shot in the ankle by an arrow, and even to share with antiquity the strange cup from which we, too, drink. This gift for transcending the usual, enriching the usual, intensifying the usual, elaborating the usual, gives it special recognition and loosens it from the constraints of familiarity.

Updike's stretching of ordinary boundaries is common to novelists, who create opportunities for exercising their own internal diversity. For them, the projection of their own characteristics onto their casts of characters is not as obvious as it is for patients who dialogue in therapy. Whether novelists are reflecting what they *are* or reflecting what they have *observed* in the world around them is arguable. Perhaps the proportions differ among writers. For those who want to, though, the chance to take their own glancing qualities and give them full personalities is abundantly available.

For Goethe, for example, to play out both the Faustian and Mephistophelian sides of himself creates expressive adventure, giving living identities to otherwise abstracted qualities. To make a Faust out of the quality of exemplary scholarship and to make a Mephistopheles out of the quality of the devil is to give each quality a vividness and elaboration unavailable to simple introspection. They each play out their special roles to the hilt, leading to a denouement quite different from Goethe's own life. As this happens, the unrequited side of Faust, who has given up worldly pleasures, is fair game for Mephistopheles, who has no need to learn from Faust or to coordinate his interests with Faust's.

In therapy, the fear of one part damaging or unduly influencing another may be relieved and gratification more easily attained than in Goethe's novel. After all, the parts, being those of one person, are inextricable from one another. They have an inevitably common interest, though they might not initially realize it. The devil in you has nowhere to go but where you go and he, therefore, has a stake in your well-being. Not so for Mephistopheles, who did not have to share Faust's fate. The message is clear: We need our parts to work together rather than trying to go off on their own.

THE EMPTY CHAIR

In addition to many internal characters, each person needs to communicate with many external characters. Often these key characters are no longer available. Among those not available are people who have died, people who have moved, people who no longer seem interesting, friends from another time, people met in passing, or even a stranger who bumped you hard in a crowd. Although continued relationship is no longer possible, these people may be valid targets for leftover communication. You may, for example, feel that you should have shoved back when the unknown person shoved you and may need to "say something" to that person. With certain people who are still available, external dialogue would be just too difficult — you might not want to confront an 85-year-old mother who ignored you when you needed her, or a touchy colleague, friend, or boss.

When such unfinished communication exists, the relevant outside person can be imagined into availability by seating him or her in the "empty chair." The patient speaks to the chair as though the other person were actually sitting in it. This option has powerful leverage, broadening the range of people with whom patients can communicate directly in a therapy session.

Novelists constantly provide themselves with this opportunity, creating characters in the mind's eye and expanding tension as the characters develop. However, while the novelist's imagined character may have no clear connection to his actual world, in therapy the person in the empty chair is clearly identified as someone with whom the patient has unfinished business.

This imagined presence was put to use in a session with Janine. Janine hated men. She had plenty of reasons, having been married to a man she thought was a horse's ass, after having been left by her father in childhood and raped in adolescence. In recent years she had walled herself off from men because for her there was no middle ground between loving them too much and cutting them out of her life. Nevertheless, she had no problem with me, seeing me more as an exception than a member of the sex. If she had found me to be one of "them," she would have had direct opportunity to face one of the hated human beings. Since I was not one of "them," the empty chair gave her a chance to try herself out with man-at-large. I asked her to imagine that the collective man was sitting in the chair. She started by vigorously moving the chair backward, setting the distance she wanted; she then went on to say what she had already told me, "I think most of you are assholes, collectively. Collectively, you treat women pretty shitty."

That was a strong beginning but the same old words. More substance was needed. The advantage of using the empty chair is that nobody immediately registers hurt and walks out. The empty chair exercise quickly allowed Janine to experience her power and her anger, where otherwise both would have remained diluted. The playing out of drama helps us get to the bare bones of any particular experience.

Then, wanting to add substance and unpredictability to the conversation, I asked Janine to sit in the other chair and become the collective man. She expressed dismay and said that I was pushing her boundaries pretty hard. I assumed she felt as though she had been asked to join the enemy camp, but I only wanted the conversation to be more palpable. In spite of her reservations Janine took the other chair. As the collective man she said, "We only do what you let us get away with." That was a point she had not brought up before, so the conversation was getting fresher. Then she returned to her chair and replied, "We don't have your birthright." She was ready to let it go at that, but the implication of an unfair advantage which women might never overcome required elaboration. I said she seemed to have more to say. She went on, "You're born with a power that we don't have when we're born, and it takes us a long time to get it. You make damn sure you don't give up much of it either." Now she had gotten across not only men's cultural advantage, but their greed in hanging onto power. She was also making sure they would feel responsible for their greed.

It is apparent that I guided Janine to a more specific dialogue than she might otherwise have created. Like any writer or editor, I had decided the dialogue needed something that she was not giving it. When she did give it more, the additional dialogue helped flesh out her introductory statement (collectively men are assholes) and aroused her to a more incisive sense of herself.

I then asked Janine to move back into the chair of the collective man. When she didn't seem to have anything further to say, I asked her, "What do you, as the collective man, think of Janine's words?" She said, "We can't help it. If we're born with it, we can't help it." This was a lame response — but it was not necessary at this point in the exercise for the villain to have his best answers available. There was enough there to accentuate his arrogance and disregard, which fit Janine's view of the collective man.

She moved back to her own chair and said with a certain sour recognition, "Why should you want to help it?" Then in his chair she said, "We shouldn't want to help it. What did I ever do to you?" In actual encounter she might have acceded to this disavowal of responsibility by men, who with easy dismissal would have made her feel she didn't have a leg to stand on. But she would have seethed internally. In this free environment, where her own authorship reigned, she felt bold enough to say, "Just about everything there was to do to me." Again, good editing required her to specify, so I said, "chapter and verse." "My father, the guy who raped me when I was 16," she went on, "the asshole that I married, who beat me up all the way." Then she said to me, "I don't think he wants to talk about that", gleeful to have cornered these men and their evasive techniques.

This dialogue was a significant advance for Janine. Still, I asked her to find out whether he did want to talk about it and then to move into the other chair and see what he had to say. He said, "I'm really sorry. I didn't do any of those things." She moved back to her own chair and stuck to her guns, saying, "Yes you did." Seeing her jaw firm up, I asked whether she could feel the sensations in her face. This was important because the feelings would add a sense of reality to her words. She could. I suggested she let those feelings be a part of what she would say. As she concentrated on the feelings in her chin, the words aroused were, "I'd like to punch you out. But I'm tired of being angry."

At this point Janine diverted her eyes from the collective man and looked at me. I directed her back. When she addressed him straight on, it became clear what she had been avoiding. She started to cry, saying in despair, "This is what I guessed. I don't want to cry." I explained that was part of it and she could go on anyway. But she was stopped. Since she needed some backing, I asked, "Do your tears stop you from telling him how pissed you are? Speak even though you're crying, even though you're pissed."

Here is a crucial point. At the very moment of experiencing her possibility for expressing herself deeply, she faced the dreaded contradiction between being strong, on the one hand, and crying, which meant weakness. She had to find out that she could cry and still have her strength and her validity. In fact, it would become a wet strength rather than the dry and mechanical strength which she saw in men. Then she said, "None of you are ever going to do it to me again. I know that. I know how not to be your victim anymore. And I have as much power as you do." There was no question that she meant every word of it and that she was no longer speaking from a one-down position. By this time her tears no longer felt weak even to her. But after her harsh words she felt sad. Even though she did not want to remain alienated, she was afraid to give up her anger lest she become vulnerable again. Once she recognized she did not, in fact, feel vulnerable, she was free to joke and laugh, with confidence. The collective man disappeared.

SEVEN

Spotlighting

(The writer) has to light up with his expressions worlds
which may never have been lighted before.

—Anais Nin

IN SHOW BUSINESS the spotlight is used to enhance the performer, enabling the audience to see her clearly and blotting out all distracting visual experience. The mind has a similar capacity, directing and simplifying human attention. This mental spotlighting may be accomplished by many simple devices. A glowing introduction, for example, will spotlight a speaker; a nickname will spotlight a personal characteristic; a title will spotlight a person's job; and black clothes will spotlight ivory skin. Opportunities for such enhancement are provided through diverse means: (1) word emphasis, (2) recognition, (3) style, (4) context, and (5) consequences.

WORD EMPHASIS

A young woman had lunch with a man slightly older and more professionally experienced than she. He said he would pay for the lunch because he had more money. She responded that he could pay if he wanted to "but not because I am poor." What she spotlighted with this choice of words was her independence *in the face of being poor.* Though her independence was admirable, the fact was that she was not poor at all; she earned $35,000 a year. Perhaps she skimmed over her affluence because she didn't want to show it off. Unfortunately, she also did it because it was her habit to see herself as poor. Upon recognizing this, she realized that it was time to stop playing poor and to feel herself an equal among the grownups.

The spotlighting power of words is especially apparent in novels, where words are used to highlight what in real life might be only an image from the past. Witness the account of E. L. Doctorow's hero in *Loon Lake.* Joe, who as a youth had been addicted to delinquency and misery, reports the apex of his early career, robbing the poorbox and kicking the balls of the fat priest who caught him. The Father goes down engulfed in spasms, gasping for air. Here is how Joe narrates the finale of the event:

> "I aim truly and he's no priest going down now with eyes about to pop out of his head, red apoplectic face I know the feeling Father but you're no father of mine he is on his hands and knees on the stone he is gasping for breath. You want the money I scream take your fucking money and rearing back throw it to heaven run under it as it rains down pennies from heaven on the stone floor ringing like chaos loosed on the good stern Father. I run through the money coming down like slants of rain from the black vaults of heaven."

This spotlight is surely aimed — at an event which is both incongruous and stunning. The event is the base to which the reader's attention is drawn, and in Doctorow's hands, it is raised into ascendancy. If, instead of writing these words, Doctorow had simply said that Joe had stolen some money from the church and lost it while running away, much of the color would have disappeared, diminishing the impact of both Joe and the priest as characters.

This disappearing act, altogether unacceptable for the skilled writer, is commonplace among people who come for therapy.

Their shame and the complexity of living through as much as they do lead to an opaqueness about experiences. I recall one person in a therapy group who lived through experiences as extravagant as Joe's but who was loath to be in the spotlight. Her words normally were the bland words of someone whose words didn't count. When, at last, she told us that as a child she had accidentally chopped her brother's finger off, her words took fire. The word "chopped" made her tremble and snapped us to attention. She told us about her shame as her mother "rushed" the boy off to the hospital, leaving her behind. Alone, she felt "ostracized" and "shivered out of my skin" over what she had done. Once her words turned the beam onto her experience, she was able to go on, welcoming us to her Gothic childhood, including her strange mother, a transvestite.

When shame and complexity suppress the experiences of most people, novelists and therapists must provide the words that inspire clear vision into the events that matter. Everybody has hurt somebody and feared the effects; everybody knows peculiar people; everybody has been left behind, feeling abandoned. Normally, these experiences remain unconscious, identified only with hazy symbols, but Annabel took a chance and said the words that would illuminate. We all know we could do the same according to our own individual circumstances.

RECOGNITION

Underground existence, insufficiently lighted, may be the destiny of most people, in spite of a personal imperative to be recognized. We see examples of this imperative early, in the attention-getting behavior of young children and in the institutionalized show-and-tell days of nursery school and first grade. Through show-and-tell, children present themselves to classmates and teachers and appreciate one another nonjudgmentally. During this exercise, there are guarantees that no person will have to fight for the attention which is widely sought and only narrowly received outside the classroom. The events of a vacation, a gift received, a discovery made, a party attended—all are given recognition. Less likely to be offered to the group because they are negative are the reports of a scolding, a forbidden wish, or a disappointment.

Such orchestrated devices as show-and-tell would be unnecessary if people were able to engage the full attention of others and have their experiences recognized. Plainly, however, many people fail to move to the foreground and forsake their sense of personal validity. Even so, in everyday life we show-and-tell all the time. Telephone calls, lunch conversations, letters, parties—all are filled with accounts of personal experience. These offerings are one of the major adhesives of community, bridging interpersonal boundaries and bringing people together. Just as two eyes give depth to vision, recognition by other people provides dimension to individual living.

The pursuit of recognition is evident in groups—professional associations, business organizations, social clubs, even families. People receive recognition by initiating ideas, by becoming spokespersons, by getting elected or chosen for positions of influence, or by functioning as contributing human beings. To be given credit for these attributes is a commonly desired form of personal spotlighting. A simple experiment with applause will accent the results of recognition. When I have asked people to stand up individually in front of a group, say their names, and listen while the group applauds for a whole minute, they have all had remarkable reactions. Surprisingly, it is about all they can bear to allow this joy to be pumped into them. Oddly, the applauders are also enthralled by doing it. The applause is compelling to both in spite of being contrived, because it sparks a fundamental need—to acknowledge and to be acknowledged.

Serving this need for acknowledgment, people celebrate births, weddings, graduations, anniversaries, promotions, retirement, and death. These personal milestones mark the trip through the years. There are countless other opportunities: a bottle of champagne for a friend moving into a new home, a toast at dinner, a letter of thanks for a gift, a special visit to a friend, or a poem written in appreciation. Still, these opportunities, more or less formal, would leave numerous dry spells in between if they were the primary sources of acknowledgment. Fortunately, opportunities for acknowledgment abound in the normal course of living—through natural perceptions of one another, through opinions about each other, through the feelings expressed when people converse, and through successes in working together. In his book *Working*, Studs

Terkel has explored the acknowledgment exercised by people from
all walks of life through their awareness and appreciation of how
they live and work. Here is the perceptive commentary by one of
them, a construction worker:

> "There's a certain amount of pride—I don't care how little
> you did. You drive down the road and you say, 'I worked on
> this road.' If there's a bridge, you say, 'I worked on this
> bridge.' Or you drive by a building and you say, 'I worked
> on this building.' Maybe it don't mean anything to any-
> body else, but there's a certain pride knowing you did your
> bit.
>   That building we put up, a medical building. Well, that
> granite was imported from Canada. It was really expen-
> sive. Well, I set all this granite around there. So you do this
> and you don't make a scratch on it. It's food for your soul
> that you know you did it good. Where somebody walks by
> this building you can say, "Well, I did that.'"

In this man's position recognition is uncommon. He knows his
own contribution but it is not often apparent to others. Although
he feels pride on his own, the warmth inside requires joining with
others in the telling of his good work. Taking accomplishment for
granted makes it fade into a pallid normalcy. Under Terkel's guidance, however, the mini-heroic was given a well-earned shot of
attention. There are many tribulations in the course of any work
project, often overshadowing personal pride and pleasure; this
time, however, self-realization and appreciation stood clear.

Troubles also require acknowledgment. Here is another of
Terkel's people, a former cop turned fireman, giving expression to
the dismaying realities of his world and an appreciation of the
people around him. He says:

> " . . . I started seein' the problems of people. Ten people in
> an apartment and there's no place to go except sit out on
> the street drinkin' beer. I guess I got this feeling from my
> father.
>   "My father's a great man. I see what he went through

and the shit and hard times. I don't see how he lived
through it. I used to lay awake when I was drinkin' and
listen to him talk all night. And I used to cry. He talked
about the shittin' war, all the money goin' for war. And the
workers' sons are the ones that fight these wars, right? And
people ain't got nothin' to eat. . . . I tell ya, if I didn't have
any income comin' in. . . . These kids hangin' around here,
Irish kids, Italian kids, twenty-five years old, alcoholics,
winos. One guy died of exposure. He went out with my
kid sister and he's dead now."

This man's desperation and clenched rage are evident. There is
also wisdom, proportion, and compassion in him, and though the
plight of the poor is hardly news, when he tells about his he
becomes the center of his bedeviled world. For the moment,
whether or not he has any control over this world, he is the authority and knows the truth of his vision. That may be slight consolation in the face of his own impotence when it comes to changing
anything. But on the smaller scale of his directly personal life, and
through his appreciation of his surroundings, he salvages a degree
of validity from the misery.

In spite of the common worship of independence, people know
themselves not only through an internal gauge but also by how
others react to them. Such external spotlighting is given a bad
name because people obviously put too much stock in what others
think of them. The resulting conformity can crop up in the most
surprising places. For example, a friend attending a large meeting
was the only person wearing a tie. Someone, spotting the tie, said,
"You're so conformist." This absurd failure to recognize uniqueness
illustrates the kind of errors of recognition which threaten the
accuracy of one's self-knowledge. Suppose a man says about you, "I
saw you on the street yesterday and tried to get your attention but
I couldn't. You are a very determined person." What he saw was a
tightness around your eyes, an urgency of stride, an angling forward in purpose—and, presto, you are said to be a determined
person. Is that what you are? Actually, you may have been preoccupied, not determined. Or you may have been late for an appointment and feeling harried. When one is wrongly acknowledged it

blurs the picture or negates the reality of one's experience. Conversely, if the observer's comment is accurate, it will add validity to the original experience and strengthen the union with him.

Illustrating the value of accurate recognition, a person in a video taped therapy session complained about her mother, saying she was so dominating as to be ludicrous. When asked to play out this image of her mother she did so in a highly aggressive tone, though in her own voice she was quite passive. She preferred the high energy she produced while playing her mother, but she believed her own voice to be more sensitive and respectful. In viewing the tape later, she saw her rendition of mother as strong, not ludicrous, and her own voice as that of a "wimp," not the sensitive person she had imagined. The tape playback flipped her out of her halo of passivity and into a new perspective on energetic freedom.

Another person, a friend, was embarrassed to tell me about her long workdays. Long indeed, starting at 5:30 in the morning and stretching well into the evening with lectures, TV appearances, meetings, etc. Although she appeared worried on this occasion, I knew she loved her hectic life and she typically looked rosy and exhilarated. When I told her I thought her work regimen was great, she was surprised, since she was expecting disapproval. Then she was able to tell me, as though confessing to a fellow conspirator, that she wouldn't want anything less demanding. Except for her vague guilt that she was doing something wrong, she regretted not one moment of her work. My words acknowledged her private truth and enriched it.

My friend's privacy was important to her, but when I recognized her she no longer needed it. Although privacy is necessary, even beautiful, when it is chronic it may be as confining as a prison cell. Therefore, a generous person spotlights another's behavior. This is accomplished when we say things like, "I didn't know it was that important to you," "just what you would say," "I never question your sincerity," or "I'm glad you came." Such ordinary remarks are the small recognitions which add up over the years. They create the confirmation and distortions which may either accentuate our own actualities or, contrarily, skew us toward erroneous awareness.

The art form of caricature is a special kind of personal recognition. Certain characteristics are presented out of context and given disproportionate attention. This can be a painful experience because the highlighting of one characteristic distorts the wholeness of the person. The purpose of the caricature—whether disparagement or humor—is important. A long-toothed political figure may be drawn with fangs, getting across the dangerous and insinuating image of a serpent. Other caricatures may express loving recognition, even when the emphasized characteristic is not particularly desirable.

Jokes can be recognitions as well. Joking about someone's inevitable lateness, recognizing a friend's one-track sexual allusions, referring to a cousin's invariable sentimentality, or exaggerating someone's generosity, courage, arrogance, energy, inventiveness, or patience—all give special focus, even though they should not be mistaken for full characterization of the targeted people. Among friends, where it is clear that the full range of the person is never lost, making one feature salient may be fun. Of course, wariness about misrepresentation takes the fun out of it for some people. But security may come through confidence in one's own wholeness and through the trustworthiness of the relationship.

Fame is another level of recognition. Actors, athletes, government leaders, artists, and adventurers are obvious recipients of mass attention. So compelling is the need for spotlighting that it fuels ambition and countless daydreams. Many people will undergo the most severe strains to achieve fame, showing no better sense than the experimental rat who goes for the pleasures of cocaine while starving to death. It was apparent during the presidency of Jimmy Carter that although he had "won" the election from Gerald Ford, thereby achieving much greater spotlighting than Ford, he was actually the loser if personal well-being were taken into account. He aged greatly in appearance, was continually attacked, often looked foolish, and had the lives of millions of people depending on the wisdom of his decisions. Yet, he wanted to run for another term!

Fortunately, fame can be scaled down. A Polish actor in the hilarious movie, "To Be or Not to Be," was said to be "world famous in Poland." All of us can become world famous in our own community of friends or family, in our factories and schools, or in the small town or neighborhood in which we live. We thus experience centrality while keeping our risks down. The experience of belonging, right in the middle of one's special world, is available to everybody. To be remembered, to be invited, to be described, to hear a story about ourselves gives most of us a flash of confirmed existence. Parents feel famous in the eyes of their children; friends in the eyes of those who appreciate them.

STYLE

In a recent movie, "Author, Author," a woman has left her husband and child and he has come after her. She screams at him; he, in turn, makes a humorous comment. She says, "It's not funny." He says, "You scream and I make jokes but we're both miserable." Her screaming makes her misery clear but his joking obscures his. Later, when the husband is trying to carry his wife bodily back home, she tells him he apparently has not noticed what has long been obvious — that she has children and leaves them, that she gets married and leaves her husbands. Her style was clear to her, but her husband had failed to give it the necessary recognition.

All people allow certain characteristics to predominate. When these characteristics become dependably recognizable, they form a person's style. Some people, for example, will always notice when someone is scornful of them but not notice when they themselves are scornful. People with a depressed style will not notice those moments when they could be pleased. Still others, who are status conscious, may not take pleasure when low-status people admire them or appreciate what is noteworthy about these people.

There is the example of a graduate student who, after a year in therapy, told me of his astonishment when one of his exams received great attention from his professor. She read it out loud to the class and wanted to make a copy of it so she could keep it. What should have been familiar praise to the student was a source of wonder instead.

This young man had been doing two things to thwart such acknowledgment. First, until now, he had always spoken with hesitation, no sentence flowing without pauses. Secondly, while talking he always looked quizzical, as though doubtful of what he had just said. When stylistically he was "saying" that he didn't know anything, it was harder for others to notice that he did. Once he began to speak less hesitantly and questioningly he was at last able to attain the recognition he much earlier deserved. Such recognition meant more to him than a ticket to an ego trip. It was a way of getting up-to-date with the truth about himself. The young man's parents had stylistically noticed only the negative about him. He knew he was better than their appraisal, yet for a long time he couldn't surmount the image.

Context

The heightening of attention may be strongly affected by the context in which it occurs. Suppose, for example, you read in the newspaper that John Smith made his first solo flight. That, by itself, has little spotlight value. If the news squib says John Smith is the first paraplegic to fly a solo flight, your interest rises. If you yourself are a paraplegic, the spotlight value is even more magnified.

More complex than this example is the following, in which Gail Godwin spotlights the lost part of a tooth. In her novel, *A Mother and Two Daughters*, Godwin writes: "There was nothing like a lost tooth, or even a piece of one, to remind you that old Father Time was chip-chipping away at the cherished edifice of self. She [Cate] wondered if Taggert McCord [who had committed suicide] had died with all her teeth intact. Or were there some bridges or gaping holes, each signaling a further erosion of confidence in herself?" The chipped tooth, a small matter by itself, becomes pivotal when placed in the context of self-esteem, aging, and suicide. Through these connections, the chipping of a tooth becomes worth the spotlight.

Psychotherapists commonly evoke context. One person, Ginny, tells about a rainy day auto accident and says she is still shook up a week later. She speaks weakly, shedding tears, and it is not clear why the effect of this minor accident lingers. But as Ginny warms up, it turns out that this accident reminds her of another, years ago. She, a social worker, was driving a 13-year-old boy—also on a rainy day—to his parents' home when she passed through a stop sign that was obscured from view. A truck hit her car and the boy was killed. Now the experience of the old accident highlighted the psychological implications of Ginny's present disturbance. She had never reconciled herself to the fact that the crash was entirely accidental. She had always—thanks to the periodic accusations of her parents—thought herself "a klutz." The two accidents cemented her klutziness.

Another client, Alice, complained to her therapist of a stiff neck. It bothered her frequently. One might think this information was not worth much, beyond compassion for another's minor pain. Yet, the alert psychotherapist will explore the complaint, believing in the fertility of the ordinary. Alice grew up as an army brat, subjected to severe discipline. Sitting properly, that is stiffly, looking straight ahead, and asking no questions were central planks in her educational program. When she was asked by the therapist to swivel her neck around, to explore how this movement would affect her, a surprising thing happened. She glanced at the office ceiling and without thinking asked if the beams were real or fake. Normally this would have been a bold remark for her and the observation itself unlikely if only she had kept her neck still. Instead of retracting or ameliorating her comment, however, she started to laugh, accepting her successful impudence with delight. Her stiff neck, spotlighted by the therapist, had been released into movement, and then, paradoxically, disappeared.

In everyday life it is difficult to extract the context which might help spotlight what is happening. To do so might be too personal or take too long. One doesn't normally ask people to start twisting their necks around to see what it's like. Yet, there are more easily recognizable aspects of the context to which one may unintrusively respond. A man calls and tells me he is going into pediatric practice. By itself this would not be especially noteworthy. But this man, my friend, has been out of clinical practice for 20 years, and such a decision will turn his life around. From this context I can join him enthusiastically as he talks about his new prospects.

Or suppose I call another friend and ask what she is doing. She is ironing her son's shirt, seemingly an ordinary act. However, I know her son has only one arm and no matter how neatly she irons his shirt some of the neighborhood kids will see him as "different" and keep their distance. While I am aware of her optimism and love, I am also sad and her otherwise ordinary words gain poignance as they reach my ears.

CONSEQUENCES

A jet plane crash will gain immediate nationwide attention. Although most events do not have such obvious and far-reaching consequences, they all contribute to the future. The more recognizable that contribution is and the more important the consequences are, the more highly spotlighted the experience will become.

Since much of what happens does not announce its consequences, both the therapist and the novelist must enhance events with consequence. Some consequences may be recognized mainly in retrospect. Lincoln's log splitting, for example, gained importance as it enhanced his reputation much later as a folksy president. But what about the everyday person? Although consequentiality is a natural part of life, any individual tends to overlook much that could prove valuable. Suppose, for example, that a person on a deserted beach starts singing. Before long he may invent some pleasant new melodies as he walks along. But when he returns home or to work, his moment of musical composition may be forgotten. It seems an isolated event without a future. An author would not allow such inconsequentiality. He wants to notice just such happenings and to find a place for them in his character's future. For him, this musical moment may lead his character to a crucial choice of new friends or to despair about the rut he is in or to a resolve to compose songs and write them down.

One of the therapist's prime concerns is to have what happens during therapy sessions change life on the outside. Many patients do not easily see these connections. One woman was stalemated with her husband whenever they disagreed, which they did all the time. She disagreed with me too; every slight divergence turned into hostility. She had gone through childhood and adolescence with her opinions cast aside, but as an adult she was stubbornly unwilling to have her views disregarded. Her disagreements with men, as well as with her husband, caused her great agitation, as she invariably felt misunderstood and demeaned. Gradually, she was able to recover from her grapples with me and laugh about sticking up for herself. She saw no connection, though, between this laughter and her prospects with her husband. When I emphasized that her pleasurable resolution with me was good practice for life with her husband, she, of course, disagreed, but laughed, realizing she was doing it again. Her laughter, however, was a sign that if she could allow resolutions with me, she might do likewise with her husband.

Consequences are not all plusses, of course. When, for example, the dire aspects of getting fired from a job are spotlighted, the person may fall into a state of apathy. But dreaded consequences fortunately are not as strictly foreordained as many imagine, and one can increase the range of possible consequences to brighten the sense of depressive inevitability. Some things, it will be realized, are more nearly inevitable than others.

EXCESSES IN SPOTLIGHTING

Although spotlighting brightens experience, it is also difficult to live naturally when the spotlight is always on. Reconciling the requirements of this special attention with the need for privacy is a constant challenge for those on center stage. In a television interview, Laurence Olivier described this paradoxical predicament when he spoke about the actor reading a review of his performance. Lord Olivier observed that the actor must guard against enlarging the review's effect and later playing it in a self-conscious and inflated manner. Yet, it would be a loss not to benefit from the review. The reviewer gives the actor invaluable information, even inspiration, to continue building on the performance. If the actor resists imitation of what was praised—or intimidation by what was criticized—he may create it afresh and relish the nuances in subsequent performances.

The same complication, on a smaller scale—suppose a man dashed out to meet his friend's car every time the friend picked him up to play racquet ball. One day the friend told him he loved the childlike way he ran out to the car. Our man was pleased at the time but for weeks felt self-conscious about "showing off" his enthusiasm and gave up running to the car. When he finally did it again, he felt natural but with a new dimension. A pleasure of which he had originally been unaware had become part of an innocent action.

Life in the spotlight can also distort the wholeness of one's reality. People are often so enticed by amplified existence that they lose the connection between amplified moments and the common moments of living. The war hero, for one, must in spite of adulation still know what it is like to eat fresh corn, struggle through university training, keep an appointment, and brush his teeth. The same applies to the person who has flunked out of school and must transcend his disgrace. People have to rise above the compulsion to live as though that which is spotlighted is all there is.

Psychotherapists, in particular, must take this compulsion into account because of the very high focus of their work. Therapists frequently believe they know their patients when actually all they know is a narrow, though highly important, part of patients' lives. I have often been surprised to see great differences in patients who move from individual therapy to a therapy group. Also surprising is how different they are when I see them for one reason or another outside the office. A person in the therapy office who is concerned about lifelong acne may well be a trusted workman in whom other people confide, a shy person in the therapy office may be a great dancer, a voluble person in the therapy office may say little at a conference.

The result of the spotlighting phenomenon may be a fixed picture. When this happens, there is a stiff self-image and a repetitious existence. In order to command a validity *beyond* any single moment or any single personal characteristic, the spotlight — which illuminates only what it points to — must be moved around to create new patterns, like a kaleidoscope. When it doesn't shift freely, people are hooked into believing only a selective part of the truth. This partial truth is often noxious, as the chronic beliefs of people in psychological trouble show. People have to find out they are more than creeps, that death is not necessarily right around the corner, or that their marriage goes beyond a failure to agree about the children's discipline.

EIGHT

Fascination

> Yet on good days Koestler radiated a rare passion for life, a deep merriment in the face of the unknown. He seemed to exemplify Nietzsche's insight that there is in men and women a motivation stronger even than love or hatred or fear. It is that of *being interested*—in a body of knowledge, in a problem, in a hobby, in tomorrow's newspaper. Koestler was supremely interested.
>
> —George Steiner

ONE PATIENT, coming into my office as someone else was leaving, asked, "When do you rest?" I told him I rested while I was working with *him*. He laughed at the repartee but there was more truth than humor in it. Through my fascination with him, my work was easy and restorative, like an automobile battery which recharges when the motor is running.

That is not to say that I was there for the entertainment, neglecting the problems he had come there to untangle. However, with fluid absorption in everything he said to me, my mind ticked off freely—without much technical intermediation—spontaneously tuned in to those therapeutic concerns he came with. Many other people will not allow me to be so easily fascinated.

They hide what would be interesting. It is part of the therapist's art to see in spite of his patient's obscuring manner.

In addition to easing relationships and restoring energy, fascination offers a greater contribution. It is a key to productivity. It is necessary for excellence in any endeavor, be it plumbing or running the family business. It funnels attention. It stokes ingenuity. It recognizes facts. It organizes tactics. It produces emotional reward; it is even its own reward. It unites experiences. It eases one moment's experience into the next, like a bird singing note after note, like an animal running stride after stride or like a new baby guilelessly shifting from one observation to another. Fascination inspires prodigious learning, indefatigable work, glorious sex, graceful movement, scientific discovery, and novel chains of ideas.

In spite of these benefits, there is an enduring struggle between human fascination and those cultural priorities which at best keep fascination "advantageously" directed and at worst obliterate it. The results of these dulling complications are faced everyday by the therapist, as well as by the novelist, as they draw material from the swings between suppression and escape. Many people wind up characteristically flat while others may be only selectively engrossing. The latter, though often interesting, may be quite unwilling to join the therapist where the interest would call out crucially shunned memories, feelings, language, or intention. Thus, in special areas of concern some otherwise fascinating people will become opaque.

Where fascination is blocked by the patient's boring ways or where the interest is wrongfully directed, it is part of the therapist's craft to recreate interest. Working against the patient's protective coloration, the therapist derives leverage through keen recognition of the patient's disregarded qualities. What is especially surprising is that accurately sensitive, clearly directed, and engrossed attention will often beget a feeling of *entrancement* in the patient. This spell-casting attention will more or less free the patient from his usual barriers, giving the therapist *entrance*, trancelike, into the private regions of the patient's mind. Under the influence of such openmindedness, to be described more fully in the next chapter, the hints sent by the patient will turn into the hunts that would uncover the overlooked episodes around every corner.

Think of the patient who sits stiffly, as though he were a ramrod, uninteresting to the casual observer—or even to himself. The therapeutic connoisseur may see that, among other possibilities, the rigid musculature is a tip-off of great physical strength or endurance. This person looks strong enough to toss the therapist's desk right through the window or enduring enough to survive years of ostracism. Another patient may speak deflatedly only about minutiae he himself doesn't care about. The therapist's attention may ease him into accounts of disappointment or abuse. In still another patient, the therapist may see a dead swelling in the face and devise a way to usher in a freer, flow of blood, or he may see hips that are soldered to legs and suggest what those legs might do. He may see a stingy demeanor and guess what the person is saving himself for; he may see a flaccid lower lip and imagine feelings of idiocy; he may hear heavily draped language and incite vulgarity.

Dave, a young engineer, was one of those people who was more interesting than he knew. He had long ago given up on himself as an interesting person, but the definitive blow came when his wife no longer wanted to be married to him. When he came to see me he had been separated from her for six months and was already living with another woman. Yet he experienced general malaise and could not get his former wife out of his mind. The obsession with her spoiled everything he did.

When Dave was young his parents traveled a lot, leaving him with housekeepers. His parents were unusually self-centered and pathologically disregarded him. They still do. However, he didn't realize they were self-centered. He just thought he was uninteresting. He was so deeply branded with this conclusion that he couldn't remember anything he had ever done which might be interesting to others. It was easy for me to see otherwise. One day, in discussing his work as an engineer, he was able to concede that he himself was very interested in—even fascinated with—his own work. He thought this was only his private interest, however, not interesting enough to others for him to tell them about it. When I asked him what they might ordinarily be interested in, he said, "recreation." Not surprisingly, he didn't think his own recreational activities worth telling about, so he kept them to himself, too. He scuba dives, which does have a romantic flavor, even for my land-lubber mentality. Here is our ensuing conversation:

DAVE: Mostly I go scuba diving with one partner, Oscar; he works on the same floor where I work. And we primarily dive along the coast here. We like to get abalones when they are in season, and lobster; that season just ended. It is really nice. You get great seafood and enjoy diving at the same time. I just get a big kick out of going down anywhere, without any goal in mind.

Notice the many hints of interest which would normally slide by, unregistered. First, he started off with an allusion to intimacy and specialness with Oscar. Then he proceeded to his knowledge-ability where few people know much. He spoke pleasure words: "really nice," "enjoy," "big kick." He also added his freedom from purpose, even a touch of adventure. He liked telling this and I liked hearing it. But he was no connoisseur and it all rolled off him. I didn't intend to let that continue. Exercising the connoisseurship he lacked, I followed my curiosity further:

ERV: Do you catch lobster with your hand, a net, or what?

Since I knew little about scuba diving, I actually wanted an answer. He could feel my interest and it opened him to an expansion of detail, moving beyond the abstractions of what is or isn't worth telling. My obvious fascination with the details was a lubricant for him; beginning to catch my interest, even awe, his words took on greater color:

DAVE: Yeah, your hand. You have to catch them with your hand. We haven't been diving that long; this was the first winter that we tried to get lobster. We initially tried to do that during the daytime, which is very difficult, because they hide under the rocks and they scoot back the minute you disturb the water. So, it is very difficult to grab them. But if you go at night, they are all out crawling around and if you shine a light at them they tend to freeze. And they move much more slowly than they do during the daytime. We tried going at night, which was great.

The action has now increased, with some graphic words about the contest he was in and the behavior of lobsters. Darkness, flashlights, scooting, hiding, difficulty, crawling, freeze all add dash to the event. His knowledgeability and innocence are also apparent again and form an interesting contrast with each other.

ERV: Do you have to go underwater to get them?
DAVE: Yeah. We usually get them at about, it varies, most successfully at about 60 feet. Night diving turned out to be a great experience. There is a lot of phosphorescence, the bubbles would be all green.

I could feel his excitement grow; even he referred to it as a great experience. Not that he had never felt this before, but now it was unnecessary for him to gloss over it. In his account he was not only doing what was interesting but also acknowledging it, which helps to make it stick.

ERV: Can you see underwater at night?

I was surprised you could. I was naive and he could teach me. The role reversal was also important, as he could accept his contribution to my knowledge.

DAVE: Depends on how bright it is. With a light you can see. On a good moonlit night you can see fairly well without it. It's surprising. Then there are more different things to see at night than during the daytime. It's a great experience.

Dave was still willing to teach me in spite of my naivete. He was also continuing to acknowledge the fascination inherent to a great experience.

ERV: What kind of fish do you get besides lobster?
 (Keep going for it, Dave!)

DAVE: I don't know the names of them. There is a variety of bass, rockfish, sometimes turbot or halibut.

ERV: You catch those also!

DAVE: We have a polespear. I'm not too fond of that myself. I feel less remorseful in killing the invertebrates than killing the vertebrates. The fish are swimming around. I could do that for a meal, yeah, we do catch some of those. Oh, yes, photography, too. Underwater photography, which can be real fun. Especially when you shoot real close up, small anemones and such, which can be real gorgeous when you print the picture of it. It gets so lost that you wouldn't be able to pick it out with the naked eye.

Dave made an interesting distinction in his feelings for vertebrates and invertebrates and then added a bonus when he introduced his photography. New things kept coming. It was important that he knew what he was doing by telling me all these experiences; otherwise his habits of dismissal might reduce the impact. Often, the therapist may depend upon an experience by itself to seed the future, requiring no commentary. It is easy for anybody to slide over his experiences without taking note of their favorable implications. For people like Dave, more vulnerable than most, comments from others about the experience are often helpful. Consequently, I later told him how he had affected me. His response suggests he got the message and would let it soak in:

ERV: You seem very fresh and lively and I am getting to know you better than I previously have. I'm glad to know you this way as well as the ways I already know you—not only the abstractions of you but also the flesh and blood of you. I can see you in the water, I can see you in your wetsuit and your oxygen tank and I can see you grabbing a lobster. I can see you with your friend and I can see you using a flashlight. I can see your movement, your energy. There is a more full sense of your reality, and I would imagine it would be important to you to experience your reality beyond all the abstractions you experience about yourself. You are this, you are that, you are a man, you are an engineer, you are a son—all of these are titles, but they are not enough to give me the substance of you. You don't think it is very much and tend to disregard your actuality.

DAVE: Yeah. I am aware that when you say that I feel that way, like what should I tell you about me. Yet, when I hear someone else speak, that is what I would like to hear, too. Exactly what you said, to put flesh on them.

There is a noteworthy aftermath to this session. Even though nothing in the session seemed even remotely connected to his ex-wife and his obsessions about her, Dave never spoke to me about her again. When, after a number of meetings, I asked why I never heard about her anymore, he said she simply didn't come to mind. No cymbals clanged, there were no reverberations, yet I believe this session opened Dave's mind sufficiently to his interestingness that his ex-wife's rejection of him became irrelevant. At that point, he felt subtly free to move on with the people with whom he was involved, particularly the woman he was living with and the people at work, where he reported much excitement and success. One might well suspect that to become interesting in ways which soften one's felt deficiency is itself a restorative force.

As reported by Jay Haley, a further example showing the importance of interest is given by Milton Erickson, one of the sage psychotherapists of our age. He was interviewed by a young man, to whom he was explaining his treatment of a woman with a washing compulsion. Erickson said, "I didn't go into the cause or the etiology; the only searching question I asked was, when you get into the shower to scrub yourself for hours, tell me, do you start at the top of your head, or the soles of your feet, or in the middle: Do you wash from the neck down, or do you start with your feet and wash up? Or do you start with your head and wash down?"

INTERVIEWER: Why did you ask that?
ERICKSON: So that she knew that I was really interested.
INTERVIEWER: So that she could join you in this?
ERICKSON: No, so that she knew I was *really interested.*

The interviewer's double-take on Erickson's emphasis seemed to be an attempt to rephrase Erickson's words into something more important than the words, *really interested*. But Erickson would not be turned aside from those very simple, yet crucial words. He believed that she would not realize she was interesting to him. Probably few people were interested. But her bodywashing was certainly a remarkable phenomenon, even though she did it quite mechanistically and would dismiss its specialness.

Erickson's patient was as talented as many others in deflecting interest. Patients repeat the same old stories, look away when talking, censor their unique thoughts, and dress drably. *Patients are often more clever at being uninteresting than the therapist is in being interested*. Assuredly, the woman with a bodywashing compulsion is well on the way toward winning the game of uninterestingness, but the undaunted therapist, while probing for all the nuances of the event, also knows that full awareness of washing one's body might evoke a number of associated possibilities. Her interest, revived, might lead her to remember an old humiliation by a teacher who accused her of being dirty. Or it might recall a time when she jumped into the bathtub with her father and was thrown out. Or the simple sensations of washing, following one after the other, might give her pleasure. Or she might notice the color of her skin and feel this is really her skin. Or, or, or. There is no end to the scenario possibilities for restoring the feeling that what she is doing, she is really doing. For her to be interested and to know someone else is interested would help confirm an existence which she may have given up on.

This transformation of the mundane into the fascinating receives comparable attention from such novelists as Barbara Pym. In her *Excellent Women*, Mildred, the main character, is a dull woman, who by her own assessment behaves as though she had "no right to be discovered outside (her) own front door." Through a series of experiences she becomes a woman of individuality and excitement, not by her resolve but through new opportunities and stimulations. During most of her life, surrounded by small-minded people, she simply doesn't notice that she is a person of independent perception, hospitality to new people, and a turning mind. Meeting two strange people who move into her apartment building and who immediately like her, she is introduced to attitudes altogether foreign to the church circles where she has devotedly served. These two psychologically reckless academics, by whom she is initially intimidated, arouse deep feelings in her, as she comes to recognize in herself an intelligence capable of full engagement with them. The mouse that she was turns into a person able to see people for what they actually are. She begins to make her own choices among them and to feel her own impact on them.

What this novel accentuates is the effect achieved by the introduction of two new people into Mildred's life. These people have no intention of changing Mildred. Although they are very different from her, as well as quite self-serving, they find her interesting, as they do much of what swims in their waters. Whatever the factors are which create a new chemistry in interpersonal ensemble, Mildred is timed to include these people this time, when previously she would have shied away. Perhaps the expansion of her mind in these new circumstances originates in a coincidental readiness to change.

There is an analogy to therapy. Just as Mildred's neighbors implant new liveliness in her consciousness, so also does the therapist offer a new presence in his patients' lives. He becomes Fifth Business, a special role described in Robertson Davies' novel by the same name. He says of Fifth Business that it refers to a role in old opera or drama, wherein the player would be neither hero, heroine, confidante, nor villain. Yet, he was necessary for the purpose of bringing about the "recognition or the denouement." Davies' *Fifth Business* character is Dunstan Ramsey, who, at ten years of age, ducks a snowball which hits the local minister's wife. The snowball, intended for him, knocks her down, causing the early birth of the child inside her and opening the cork for Davies to pour out three absorbing novels about the consequent fate of several of his fictional people.

Such influence, fortuitously generative, happens in the lives of all people, but they often slough it off. The therapist is required not only to notice such influences, which give shape and direction to a person's life, but also to be Fifth Business himself. He is the new person in a patient's life, not a main character but a leverage point, giving a boost for new levels of experience. It is his task to insure that, in spite of having no primary place in his patients' lives, he is accepted by them as a marvelous addition. His special flavor of mind—insightful, respectful, humorous, fresh spoken—

may easily be overshadowed by his role as a technical instrument. He is, after all, only a temporary presence; he is only—only—a stepping-stone.

THE INTERPLAY BETWEEN TECHNIQUE AND FASCINATION

Fascination is only part of the job. It is a partner with technical savvy. For enchantment with each person to be useful it must be joined with the discipline to follow the therapeutically relevant themes. There is always an incredible number of things to be interested in; only some of them will hit the therapeutic mark. Many interesting phenomena will have little payoff. A therapist fascinated with a patient's beautiful metaphors may be distracted from his drinking problems. A lisp, a recent visit to Africa, or an auto accident seen on the way to the office may be best left to rest in peace. Or these very interests, fruitless at one moment, may pay off when attention to them is timely.

With an infinite number of such technical considerations to keep in mind, the therapist is sorely tested in keeping his mind open to simple responsiveness. Thus divided between fresh interest and a guiding methodology, the therapist's homage to his learned procedures will often distract him from a wholehearted appreciation of the many fascinating characteristics all patients bring to their sessions. Therefore, it is important that the methodology he follows includes within it a heartening guidance to therapeutically fruitful fascination. Fortunately for the discerning therapist, that is exactly what good methodologies do.

Freud, as a classic example, included some elemental sources of fascination in his psychoanalytic technology. Principal among them was free association. This strange freedom for the patient to say just exactly what was on his mind, irrespective of all common verbal requirements, was a great step into fascination. The concept of transference was also an invitation to fascination. The therapist became no less than a symbol of the most important people in the patient's life. How the patient behaved with the analyst became a key to the crucial understandings of his life. Nothing could be casual when everything that happened was a symbolic signpost to those elements from which the patient's soul was constructed. In spite of the fact that many people were quite capable of being bored even under such circumstances — analysts and patients alike — the transference implications presented an opportunity for one of the more absorbing engagements of the age.

Around 1950, gestalt therapy also constructed its own methodological inspirations to fascination. High on the list was the heavy emphasis upon immediacy of experience and upon tuning sharply into this experience. The experiences receiving high focus ranged from simple sensations, like a tightness in the jaw, to broad value systems, like wanting governmental support for the poor. It became clear that pointed notice of key happenings resulted in especially strong feelings.

Gestalt therapy further emphasized the healing powers of good quality contact, reacting strongly against the depersonalized experiences so common in the culture. Supporting improved contact were specific insights concerning the psychological value of the simple contact functions of seeing, hearing, talking, touching, and movement. The enhancement of these functions was instrumental in the further amplification of personal experience. With this amplification, high levels of fascination were created.

Advancing this emphasis on immediacy still further was the so-called *experiment,* that is, the therapeutic use of practice opportunities for any form of needed behavior. If, for example, a patient could not successfully talk to a parent, a spouse, a boss, or an old nemesis, he could practice it, usually right in the therapy session. Or, if a person was not projecting his voice well, he might be taught how to breathe more effectively. The move to immediate action created an emergency — facing the dangerous person in fantasy or practicing a risky function. The emergency was a relatively safe one since no one would be fired, ostracized, or punished, and the therapist was an expert ally. In spite of the relative safety, plenty of personal risk remained, however, and the danger created a narrow and intensified focus. Even though these risks were usually beneficial, some dangers would nevertheless be too great, so the therapist had to help keep the danger within experimentally manageable bounds.

The great fascination which accompanied these technical developments was harmonious with the then-growing requirements for fascination evident in the culture at large. Students in school began to think education should be interesting as well as preparatory; humdrum marriages were abandoned rather than endured; the market for sensation was expanded, including the sale of violence, sex, and terror; sound was amplified, color became more extravagant, etc. With all the unfortunate excesses these amplifications fostered, they nevertheless did give support to renewed self-interest in a world where resignation all too commonly seemed the only alternative.

Given the methodological supports for fascination implicit in psychoanalysis and gestalt therapy, as well as in other methods, it is only a short step to join more fully now with the novelists in making fascination explicitly central. People come to therapy not only to solve a whole range of well-documented problems, but also to restore their powers of fascination and to learn to exercise them. They already read novels with the expectation of being fascinated, and the material of fiction comes from the same reservoir of personal experience. When people come to therapy, they are faced with mysteries they can't fathom, dangers that menace them, deaths they can't get over, loves they can't satisfy, and hopes for a restoration of lost opportunities. They have strange characteristics, unique to themselves, as well as many common bonds with the therapist, including the capacities for surprise, laughter, violence and degradation. Only a jaded or distracted therapist would not be fascinated, even though the patients themselves may only experience a neutered or agonized existence.

Fascination has a subtly confirming effect upon people, because its wholeheartedness at least momentarily honors their behavior. This has nothing to do with approval of specific behavior, although the infusion of genuine interest serves as a dependable ground for mutuality. At its height the effects of fascination may be hypnotic, opening the stuck person to greater versatility. With one particular couple, Jack and Alexis, my values were altogether in conflict with Jack's, yet my fascination enabled him to continue working with me and provided an atmosphere in which he could turn his potentially tragic marriage into one which was minimally injurious to him and his wife. The two of them, together, were a burlesque. The adversarial nature of their marriage was reminiscent of the couple in Georges Simenon's novel, *The Cat*. In *The Cat*, right to the end, two embittered, stunted people play out a hatred which blankets a decayed love, leaving only the barest trace of a tenderness, too faint to matter. The wife had poisoned her husband's beloved cat. From then on silence between them was moderated only by the passing of notes and the cruel tricks they played on each other. Only at the wife's death did her husband call out her name and think longingly "there was no longer anything."

Jack and Alexis were more fortunate. They *did* come to their senses before it was too late. By the time they entered therapy, they couldn't stand each other. He was a huge, burly, red-complexioned throwback to an absurdly macho, steel mill mentality. She was a radiant, exotic looking woman he had met in Greece. She no longer even wanted to talk to him. Oddly enough, she still prepared his meals. But it was hard to tell what these two could possibly have seen in each other. She had so much energy her skin seemed stretched with it, yet in order to keep peace she determinedly reined in this energy to near catatonia. *All* she wanted anymore was peace. She tried to achieve this peace by tightening her body so intensely you could almost see her doing it. She spoke only terse words; even a sentence would be more than he deserved. Of course, this was no way to achieve peace. When she failed to iron his shorts, he slugged her. Even his fist could not get through the armor of her sardonic superiority. She had her own "machisma" and would never budge, not even if he were to maim her.

I walked over to the couch to sit next to him. With my arm on his shoulder, I asked him whether he knew what an ugly man he was turning out to be. He was incredulous that I would say that and appalled at my judgment. He told me anybody would have slugged her and that I was a pansy to think otherwise.

He was so strange, like a bull trying to eat at a dinner table. In spite of this huge difference in our attitudes, he could tell from my touch and from seeing and hearing me that I was fascinated, no less so than if I had been watching two autos colliding. What this did for him was to make it clear, without my saying so, that, despite our contrary values, I was in for the duration, like a person who couldn't put Jack's book down. He and his wife were engrossing caricatures, who for their petty resolve—each one, for example, was unwilling to give up their house to the other—would have been willing permanently to endure silence in an atmosphere of latent explosion. Jack later became less macho and left, giving up a house which meant little to him to begin with. The rigid courage of the crazy, who as in *The Cat* play out their hands monomaniacally, gave way, in this case, to flexibility and a mutually agreeable settlement.

The Cat accents the worst that could happen in a marriage, since the characters do not escape the implacability of their grudging minds. The author follows them to their destined deterioration, letting their meanness play itself out to its full extent. Nothing stands in the way for them on their trip downward. To find out what will happen when going all the way with one characteristic is a great luxury for an author. The braking effect of complexity is missing when his character's mind is consumed with only one option, and tragedy is a foreordained result. There is no one around to help the characters make their lives different—not even the author, who is only curious to see what will happen.

Jack and Alexis *could* have been the characters in *The Cat* but they were not going it alone. In the company of an external mind, they found the complexity in their lives. Heaping misery on each other seemed at first bewitchingly attractive; they could only see each other's throats. Then, at last, they cared to survive.

Their coupled ordeal was fascinating because it illuminated the risky nature of marital experience, worthy of anyone's attention. Their situation was like the stark example of *The Cat*, but they didn't have to go all the way with it before accepting the humanity of resolution. To join with them, absorbed as a witness, opened me to those humane impulses which escape the technology of cool observation. Erasmus wrote long ago of Folly, who cut through stodgy knowledge to a fascination with the simple experiences of living. He recommended a special form of flattery, more honest than the word now implies, more like fascination joined with kindness. This state of mind

> . . . proceeds from a certain gentleness and uprightness.
> . . . It supports the dejected, relieves the distressed, encourages the fainting, awakens the stupid, refreshes the

sick, supplies the intractable, joins loves together and keeps them so joined. It entices children to take their learning, makes old men frolic, and under the color of praise, does without offense both tell princes their faults and show them the way to amend them. In short, it makes every man the jocund and acceptable to himself."

With such a repertoire to substantiate it, fascination helps to avert the trivialization by technology fostered by detached expertise.

NINE

Escape From the Present

They say Ulysses wearied of wonders,
wept with love on seeing Ithaca,
humble and green. Art is that Ithaca,
a green eternity, not wonders.

—Jorge Luis Borges

To UNDERSTAND the healing influence of fascination more free-ly, it is helpful to see its relationship to the here-and-now emphasis so popular in recent years. This emphasis cuts out any distracting regard for things of the past or future or for things happening elsewhere. When these distractions are gone, a pointed experience is left, more sharp than if everything were taken into account. With such uncluttered awareness, concentration is deepened, leading each person into wholehearted function. Anybody study-ing for an exam or trying to pitch a baseball knows this and tries to erase everything else from his mind. But in spite of such earnest efforts it is hard to achieve sharp attention when there are always a million competing interests.

Around 1950, therapists became especially alert to these inter-
ferences with focus, which they found to be barriers to change.
Many of them came to distrust intricate networks of influences,
which they saw as evasions of what they thought really counted —
the things happening right now. Whereas previously therapists'
accepted subject matter included many detached lamentations
about the past, worried anticipation of the future, and empty accounts of rejection by friends, in the new approach they became
intent on cutting through all the psychological red tape and getting down to clear sensations and feelings. When they were able
successfully to funnel the events from a vast psychological landscape into the present, they found this to have a purifying effect.
In a world gone haywire with complexity, the accent on immediacy
underscored simplicity and helped close off many of those debilitating habits of mind which made therapy slow going.

In this narrowed mode, any single point of keen concentration
might trip off a chain of internal events. A simple sensation like an
itch, for example, when receiving such focussed attention, might
at first get stronger. Then it might move to another area of the
body, then another, then back to the original place. In continued
concentration each awareness might ignite the next until the
whole body would be warmed as though with a soft fire. The
growth of sensation might come like dominoes rising instead of
falling down, collecting waves of feeling which released pent-up
energy, invigorating the person who originally only had an ordinary itch that could be ignored.

Such fascination with simple sequences of sensation was also
available in more complex behaviors. Here-and-now dialogues with
a visualized father were more dramatic than conversations *about*
him, hitting pillows was more engrossing than telling about un-
fought battles, and openly expressing held-back criticism out-
stripped allusions to vague grievances. These, as well as many
other exercises in immediacy, led many people into previously
unimagined highs in fascination, and a new term, peak experience,
was adopted as a code word for total absorption and its scintillating
consequences.

The impressive effects of *concentration* were overshadowed by a widespread belief in what was *spuriously* identified as the power of the present. The here-and-now orientation does not by itself assure high quality concentration. Many people have poor powers of concentration even though they may be immersed in their current concerns. Depressed persons, for example, are little concerned with the future and only mistily concerned with the past. It is their concentration, not their calendar, which is flawed. Nor do people with good concentration stay focused on the present. Obviously, their interests may range to events which happen in any place or any time.

Nevertheless, since it was easier to say *now* than to teach people *how* to concentrate, the instruction to stay in the present caught on more readily than the more intricate requirements of concentration. There was a swelling number of people who endorsed the idea of living in the present, as they realized how much they had lost by allowing their lives to be delayed and deflected. For them to put life on the back burner until some future time when they would graduate or get married or retire was understandably no longer acceptable. Many people came to believe that the present was all they had in life, the only reality.

Even as recently as 1984, this was reflected in a book cutely called *The Precious Present*. In this book, the present is unabashedly glorified. Appealing to a popular audience, the book is written in fable style. An old, wise man, explaining the Precious Present to a young boy, says, "It is a present because it is a gift, and it is precious because anyone who receives such a present is happy forever." The objectification of the present goes on as the boy searches for it as though it were the Holy Grail. Although this book creates greater deification than is common, it illustrates the key position of the "present," which has become a catchword pointing to self-sufficiency, relevance, and authenticity. However, it can also become a cramping perspective, often diminishing attention to many worthy aspects of living.

Deep concentration, only incidentally induced by instructions to stay in the present, is a skill with which everybody is born. It is a natural attentiveness, through which each person draws the surrounding world into his own experiential boundaries. When this function is working well, each person may stretch freely and gracefully toward everything within sovereignty. Adults will enviably recognize this sovereignty in young children, whose ability to be fully absorbed is, to the adult, like a dream come true. Through their simple concentration, children are easily fascinated.

As they grow older, children's interests become highly directed by others: parents, friends, teachers, religious leaders, and policemen. They are not allowed to do many of the things that arouse their interest, like crossing the street, playing sex games, dropping mother's bowls to see how they crack and break. They are also overwhelmed by shouting, spanking, and contradictory instructions. And they are required to do many things they would rather not do, like sitting in geography class or eating certain hateful foods.

Concentration and the accompanying fascination then begin to fade. In school some fortunate students remain fascinated by what they learn but most of them simply have to get the learning done. At best, they do so with grim determination or habit or with half a mind elsewhere. Nor do teachers often care whether their students are fascinated — only whether they learn the required material, be that multiplication tables, Shakespeare, or a foreign language. The message received is: Since learning can't be put off, like it or not, do it!

For many people there is nothing to do but detach to one degree or another. This is how people get through many of the things they have to do. Hold your nose while you eat brussels sprouts, tighten your muscles when you might make a mistake, daydream about a classmate instead of talking to her. It is this epidemic detachment that the here-and-now advocates were intent on eradicating. Not that detachment was anything new, accumulating, as it has been, all through the ages. In this century, however, detachment has made a special mark. It has been a theme favored by a large number of writers, particularly Kafka, Sartre, and Camus. By now, the recognition of detachment has grown so widely that it is not only extensively examined in the arts but also subject to frequent general commentary. It doesn't take much philosophical sophistication nowadays to be aware of the depersonalized forces at work.

DISSOCIATION

Concentration and detachment may be seen as polar opposites, and concentration remains difficult as long as detachment works against it. Conformity, untimely habits, faulty language, large obligations to certain people, and a variety of special fears are all included among the distracting influences everybody lives with daily. Assuming these influences will not evaporate, the improvements in concentration must come, bootstrap style, *in spite of* continuing cause for detachment. This is a convoluted problem, indeed, and the here-and-now experience took a step toward untangling it by doing one especially remarkable thing: *It made allies of concentration and detachment!* While concentrating on the here-and-now, one detaches from everything else. The here-and-now stakes out a small area for concentration as its domain. The rest doesn't count.

By such narrowing of personal focus, the emphasis on the present helped to refurbish a venerable psychological vehicle— dissociation. That is, by means of a natural dissociative capability, people are enabled to disconnect their attention from important areas of their lives so as to fix attention on some particular concern. This dissociative phenomenon used to be considered pathological because it implied a serious failure in making the necessary shifts of attention back and forth among various areas of potential concern. A person with a multiple personality, for example, when in one identity would not know of the existence of other identities. Or a person might dissociate suicidal thoughts and become driven, trance-like, to commit suicide. Actually, dissociation is not merely pathological. It is one more phenomenon that may be apparent at any point on a pathology-health spectrum. It may represent the apex of healthy fascination or a delusion in a hospital back ward.

Dissociation may thus be recognized as a common device for cutting off attention from much of what might be unwelcome. This exclusion is taking place when a driver who is daydreaming suddenly notices that he or she has given no attention to the road. Or dissociation may appear less dangerously and more purposefully when a painter is surprised to realize it is dinner time and lunch was forgotten. For this driver and this painter, shifts in attention are temporarily inaccessible. Whether the shifts in attention are desirable depends on specific circumstances. The painter, wholly fascinated with work, need not shift attention unless there is a fire or an important date elsewhere or starvation looms. Clearly, at times the dissociated attention may be effective, representing the height of single-minded attentiveness; at other times, where shifts are required, it could be disastrous.

The risk in single-minded concentration, of course, is that one may shelve many experiences which are indispensable. Sooner or later what is ignored may turn up to haunt one. Whatever one is now doing, feeling, or wanting is best harmonized with a huge background of experience from which it evolves and into which its traces recede. No idea, no behavior, no wish is an independent entity. Whether a person drinks wine, milk, water, or hemlock will be connected with what already matters to that person. Therefore, an individual who has joined A.A. will generally not drink wine, a debaucher will not drink milk, a swimmer will not drink the water he is swimming in, and a happy person, in spite of stray thoughts to the contrary, will not commit suicide.

Although there are numerous exceptions to these equations and considerable room for personal uniqueness, the ground of anybody's experience is more or less unfriendly to disharmony. It takes a lot to shake a person loose from this system of interwoven elements, which is why "you can't run away from yourself." Yet, though you can't actually run away from yourself, if you are to change you must transcend this ever present background, the influences of which have already affected your state of mind. The dissociative route, which I shall soon describe, is one powerful means for trying to bypass these influences. Before elaborating on that option, however, let me sketch the contrasting option for psychological change, one which emphasizes *context* in the evolution of anybody's life.

First, in considering the role of context, anyone can choose what matters from an essentially generous number of options, more than any one person takes advantage of. To illustrate, we may start with the realization that one cannot just see a man, period. One can only see a man who, among many other contextual possibilities, is walking on a street, wearing sports clothes, holding the hands of two children, one of whom is his son and the other his neighbor. This is a simple statement of the inevitable relationship of figure to ground; that is, in this case, of man to street, children and clothes. But the perceiver—suppose she is a woman—has other choices in linking the man who is seen and everything else that forms the context for her perception. The whole experience will be different if this perceiver is preoccupied with an unhappy phone call. She may then notice the man only casually. If, on the other hand, the perceiver herself is deeply absorbed with the man, the phone call might not matter very much. Or she may only notice the children in a peripheral way. Still further, she may feel sympathy, if she knows the man's wife recently died. Or seeing the man might awaken a flashback to a scene in a movie. Or she might want to shout out her greetings and invite the man and kids to her home. All these options from the background give the perceiver great leverage for individual choice in behavior and feeling.

Second, in emphasizing context, one may reinterpret things which have already happened, a widely recognized procedure in psychoanalysis. This option rests on the realization that undesired behavior and feelings exist because of the *context* provided by the early lives of people. For example, a patient, always in great discomfort in the presence of her employer, may have forgotten how loudly her father hollered at her. In psychoanalysis she remembers, thereby giving herself a chance to change her understanding of what actually happened in those early years. She may realize that her father's hollering sprang from desperation about troubles quite unrelated to his daughter. The newly experienced context which this understanding provides would be more hospitable for the patient's improved contact with her boss, who is after all not her father and (supposedly) not desperate. Psychoanalysts, seeing this reorganization of the past to be fruitful, naturally gave heavy emphasis to the context of each person's life.

Now, back to the dissociationists, who approached change from just the opposite position. Instead of foraging in the context, they tried more or less to abolish it and start fresh with new experience. The main methodological arenas for these explorations were brainwashing, meditation, hypnosis, drugs, and the here-and-now orientations of psychotherapy, especially those of gestalt therapy. Although each of these instrumentalities offer different motives, procedures and results, they all induce people to flip out of the time continuum. That is a magnetic prospect in a world of increasing time pressure, where a popular saying came to be, "Stop the world, I want to get off." These methods helped to do just that, guiding people to find asylum in a present that seemed pure, absorbing, all of a piece, all by itself. Let's look at how each of them developed openness to new experience and also constructed prison walls.

BRAINWASHING

Usually, dissociative procedures were administered to people who, though they might not foresee all the effects, were nevertheless willing participants. This was not always true, however, particularly in the brainwashing of people who were political deviates or foreign enemies. Brainwashing is perhaps the most harshly intentional example of the abolition of context. The aim is to create a clean slate—forcefully, if necessary—opening the mind to receive whatever is currently fed into it.

Brainwashing methods have been utilized through the ages in one form or another, but the term is currently used to describe the relatively recent workings of the Chinese and Russians in skewing people to their sociopolitical system. Here is one example of how they went about it. According to R. L. Walker, writing in 1956 about the indoctrination of Chinese workers, they started by separating their trainees for nine to twelve months from their normal locale and from the normal influences of family, friends, and activities. In American culture, we have long created new learning atmospheres for young people when they leave home for the first time to go to college. Recently, with easier mobility, we even send high school cheerleaders away from their home communities to learn their craft while living together on distant campuses. The retreat, commonplace now in churches and industry, as well as for encounter groups, is also geared to create an isolated atmosphere for optimal learning. People who go off on these quests take leaps in learning through the focused attention, which is made easier by separation from their families and other familiar influences.

Building on this isolation from the familiar, the Chinese program was also designed to create fatigue—more harshly than is customary in our retreats. They crammed in a heavy concentration of work, just as our medical schools do, leaving little opportunity for relaxation or reflection. They increased the absorption still further by escalating tension and uncertainty. The forms through which this tension was amplified were menacing. People disappeared and rumors were spread about their fate. As though this were not enough to magnify anybody's personal stake in learning correctly, vicious language served further to heighten the sense of urgency. The Chinese were apparently reading from the same page as Synanon, where vicious language has been equated with honesty and spontaneity. The crowning blow by the Chinese against the retention of ordinary proportion was to forbid humor—normally a welcome reminder that all is not exactly as it is purported to be.

Plainly this format created an emergency, which itself always funnels the mind into immediacy. These trainees found themselves in a brand new milieu, for which their customary world, temporarily at least, had little relevance. After such periods of exhaustion and crisis, "tailcutting" was said to take place, the "tails" being ties with whatever was paramount before—values, friends, family, work, pleasure preferences, etc. As William Sargent, another investigator of the brainwashing phenomenon, has said, belief systems "can be implanted in people . . . by accidentally or deliberately induced fear, anger or excitement . . . The cortical slate may be wiped clear temporarily . . . allowing (other behaviours) to be substituted."

Robert Jay Lifton interviewed a number of previous "enemies" who had passed through the Chinese thought reform process. It is again evident that a major ingredient of their experience was the subordination of context; that is, what previously mattered in each person's life was annulled. One person said about his experience, "You have to get rid of and denounce all your imperialist thoughts, and you must criticize all of your own thoughts, guided by the official. . . . This is necessary, because *if you don't get rid of these thoughts, you can't put in new ones*" (italics mine).

Although those indoctrinated will commonly become sold on the new beliefs, they are often left, when they are released, with what Lifton and others have described as the "thousand mile stare." They live disconnectedly in the old environment to which they have returned. I have seen a comparable look, not as severely disconnected, on a few encounter group devotees, who are wont to jargonize words like "I-can-relate-to-that," to hug the nearest person, or to dismiss someone by saying "that's-your-problem."

Among the graduates of Chinese programs, there is a painfully divided consciousness when they return to the west. They seem resurrected, as though from the dead. The resurrection seems a mixed blessing however, when one observes not beatitude but rote rhetoric and blank visage. Are they now restored from the effects of the imprisoned years or from the effects of the earlier years from which they had been disconnected? Between the two educational warriors, each driving to design their minds, they lie twice conquered and with debilitated allegiance. Although the Chinese reeducation "takes," some brainwashed people are newly ripped apart by the conflicting context in the west. Even when they see flaws in the indoctrination, they long for the simple compatibility between their new ideas and the prison philosophy. This compatibility between what is immediately experienced and the context in which it occurs—so necessary for internal harmony—is shattered when they now return to what may originally have been as comfortable as an old shoe.

HYPNOSIS

Hypnosis is another way to disconnect a moment of experience from the context in which it appears. Hypnotic induction methods are generally geared to narrowing the individual's focus. While varying widely in procedure and purpose, hypnotists most recognizably work by directing attention to some specific sensation or some specific external object, subordinating attention to anything else. Marion Moore has said about Milton Erickson, the best-known therapeutic hypnotist, that he was a "master at distracting people from focusing on their surroundings and their thoughts. . . . The goal of his induction procedures was to turn the person's mind inward and thus limit his attention to external stimuli. This protraction of attention would quickly stimulate a deep trance." Once the trance is stimulated and the person is in this dissociated state, normal beliefs and habits can often be bypassed. The specific new absorption by the hypnotized person takes over and serves to set aside everything else. As Erickson and his co-author, Ernest Rossi, have said, "When the therapist correctly labels the patient's ongoing, here-and-now experience, the patient is usually immediately grateful and open to whatever else the therapist may have to say. (This opens) a yes set for whatever suggestions the therapist may wish to introduce."

This description of trance induction supports the proposition that full here-and-now experience may change a person's hospitality to new ideas. Once the dissociation is created, this person is free to talk with the therapist about experiences otherwise inaccessible. Or through posthypnotic suggestion he's able to do things he would otherwise not do. Sometimes the accompanying single-mindedness sweeps patients too far forward and they balk. At other times they may move forward but become quite anxious. In either case, the therapist is faced with a limitation in his powers to abolish context altogether. In the presence of painful fears, the therapist must proceed to guide the individual through the terrors which remain in force.

One major difference between hypnosis and brainwashing is that, whereas brainwashing requires a lengthy process, hypnosis is especially noted for the tight interval between induction and the special consequences intended. In a short time the hypnotic state permits well-known effects, ranging from anesthesia and great feats of strength to remembering deeply forgotten events. Through posthypnotic suggestion a person will call a friend she was afraid to call, tell her child stories she was too shy to tell, give lectures calmly where previously they had created panic, enter an elevator which had seemed like a death warrant. These and comparably remarkable results — unavailable under ordinary circumstances — give hypnosis a secure place in any historical repertoire of the seemingly magical.

One person in a group hypnotic demonstration, having been told he would be unable to raise his arm, reported later that he knew he *could* raise his arm if he *wanted* to, but that he didn't know how to want to. For the execution of this simple move the necessary connection between his will and his instrumentality was simply missing, as though the linchpin of his character was no longer holding its parts together. Similar dissociation may happen spontaneously in everyday life. After emerging from a depressed mood, one woman told her husband that she had wanted to talk to him, even to forgive him, but couldn't find any way to open her mouth.

Another difference between brainwashing and hypnosis is that hypnosis is usually used in a specific and temporary engagement and the dissociated state is not forced on the person. However, the distinction is sometimes murky. There is a growing recognition that the factors which are so influential in the familiar hypnotic trance are actually operative on a more pervasive, even involuntary, basis. Arousals to immediacy will commonly create some level of dissociation. Saving a child from drowning, getting caught in a fight, watching a fire shoot 50 feet in the air will all cause a person to forget everything else. Other everyday experiences have a spontaneously hypnotic influence. Eloquence, tapping incisively into specific needs of people, creating a sense of emergency, supporting one's position convincingly, an aura of success are among those influences which attract high focus. Their effects do not require any of those specifically prepared conditions of attention usually qualifying an experience as hypnotic. Yet, with improved hypnotic technology and with a social atmosphere which reveres the present, there may be a growing prospect that people will be increasingly susceptible to believing that whatever is currently aroused is all there is. Hypnosis is one of the great discoveries of the ages, working not only therapeutically but also providing glimpses into secret turnings of the mind. But, to flip an old saying around, it is a good wind that blows no ill, which may be the guiding theme of this entire chapter.

MEDITATION

The wondrous leverage hypnosis promised for changing behavior has been matched by its first cousin, meditation. Sometimes they are indistinguishable from each other. They both exclude the normal range of a person's perception in favor of an enduring, undistracted attention. Meditation has become as commonplace among large numbers of people as prayer is to the churchly. Many people will repeatedly, usually daily, focus for an extended period, 20 minutes or more, on a mantra, image, sensation, frame of mind (like love), etc. From this beginning, impressive internal changes often follow. Abiding peace, a sense of cosmic harmony, bodily ease, unadorned confidence, a sprightly optimism in tackling problems — are all examples of the great leverage into personal transformations provided by meditative attention.

Gopi Krishna, a practitioner of meditation, has written eloquently about his searches into the realm of the Kundalini experience. Kundalini is a vital energy current rooted in the lower end of the spine. When awakened, it "carries the limited human consciousness to transcendental heights, endowing the individual with incredible psychic and mental powers." Krishna's experiences, of course, surpass those of the ordinary practitioner of meditation. They are luminous and rapturous. It is best to use his own words to illustrate the ecstatic powers affecting the advanced meditator. About his dream life he says,

> My dreams, which possessed a highly exotic and elusive quality, were so extraordinarily vivid and bright that in the dream condition, I lived literally in a shining world in which every scene and every object glowed with lustre against a marvelously illuminated background, the whole representing a picture of such resplendence and sublime beauty that without implying the least exaggeration I actually felt as if every night during slumber I roamed in enchanting empyrean regions of heavenly life. . . . The vivid impressions left by a well-remembered happy dream during the night lingered for the whole day, a sweet memory of what appeared to be a supermundane existence for a few hours, to be followed by that of another seen on the succeeding night as sweet and vivid as that on the previous one.

Lest such bliss be envied out of context, Krishna reports that,

> like the vast majority of men interested in Yoga I had no idea that a system designed to develop the latent possibili-

ties and nobler qualities in man could be fraught with such dangers at times as to destroy the sanity or crush life out of one by the sheer weight of entirely foreign and uncontrollable conditions of mind.

Krishna attributes the almost ruinous tortures which accompanied his released Kundalini currents to a faulty direction taken in his self-guided explorations. We might also speculate, however, that the troubles arose because of difficulties in assimilating energies for which his previous life experiences did not provide an accepting background. The new energies, dissociated, arose in spite of, not because of, important aspects of his previous life experiences. Such courage as is required for surpassing one's apparent fate was abundantly available to him, and during the course of his internal war a reconciliation occurred between Kirshna's luminosity and the life which he had previously lived. At one point, before this harmony appeared, he reported the dimensions of his loss by saying,

> I lost all feeling of love for my wife and children, I had loved them fondly from the depths of my being. The fountain of love in me seemed to have dried up completely. . . . I looked at my children again and again, trying to evoke the deep feeling with which I had regarded them previously, but in vain . . . *They appeared to me no better than strangers.* (italics mine)

DRUGS

As mind boggling as the effects of meditation may sometimes be and as widespread as its practice has become, it must nevertheless take a back seat to drugs in its potency. Drugs execute an immediate, powerful invasion of the person's mind, without any indoctrination process. With this attribute, they are made to order as an instrument of the here-and-now mentality. No waiting; once begun the deed is done. Having been entered by the drug, be it marijuana, LSD, heroin, cocaine or many others, people move into a new world of experience from which there is no turning back until the drug has run its course. Although the entry is mechanical, each person will develop his or her own unique experience. In spite of being held within the drug's sovereignty, the background of the user will still make a mark. On LSD, for example, one person may have delicious visions of otherwise unreachable combinations of beautiful colors and shapes. Another may be terrified by the threat of being swallowed by a mountain. A third may experience sexual transcendence while hunting an elephant. A barrier to personal benefit is that, while these personalized differences are pertinent to each individual's life, the person may feel that the experience is happening to him or her instead of making it happen. Some people, may discover connections with the context of their lives only in retrospect. They may then be able to use these illuminations as a guide, much as they might with dreams. Unfortunately, the personal implications usually vanish; it then just seems more compelling to get back to the drug again. In competition with ordinary life, the drug is a greater magnet, and with extended use the doors of the prison of the present slide shut.

Gestalt Therapy

Gestalt therapy takes its place among these context-shrinking instrumentalities, even though the primacy of the present was originally only a small part of its method. In spite of the narrow impressions picked up by many practitioners, gestalt therapy is a complex methodological system. A basic condition for the gestalt here-and-now is the inclusion of remembering, imagining, and planning as present functions. Although this qualifier should insure attention to any experiences, no matter where or when, it has suffered the fate qualifiers often do. It has taken a back seat. Inevitably, people are confused by the paradoxical clash between believing that the past doesn't count and simultaneously believing that remembering does count. Since paradox is hard to handle, one side has become dominant—the belief that only the present counts.

This happened even to Fritz Perls himself, the originator of gestalt therapy. In his early theorizing he described the present as "an ever moving zero point of the opposite past and future," still recognizing the past and future as live reference points for the present. Though he never actually changed his mind, one would not know this by reading his later aphorisms about the present. Whereas in his actual therapeutic work he was a master at leading people into reenactments of early life experiences, so vividly restored as to feel almost like a trip in a time capsule, he nevertheless was moved to write in *Gestalt Therapy Now*:

> I have one aim only: to impart a fraction of the meaning of the word *now*. To me, nothing exists except now. Now = experience = awareness = reality. The past is no more and the future is not yet.

What were his readers and his listeners to think? The most careful and serious among them were able to coordinate this statement with his actual work and with other of his guidelines, such as the need to finish unfinished business, the indivisible relationship between figure and ground, and the centrality of human *functions*. These perspectives all respected the diversity of experience and the context within which it was embedded. Nevertheless, for others the simplistic picture he drew of the here-and-now stood out. In the service of quick communication, the distinct equations Perls enunciated between now, on the one hand, and experience, awareness, and reality, on the other, worked well—but were only loosely accurate. Since the present is only a point on a time continuum, it is actually neither experience nor awareness nor reality. All are occurrences in time, not time, just as a jewel in a box is not a box.

A further error concerning the here-and-now was that Perls' slogans about the present were part of the spreading existentialist ethos. Actually, many existentialists, including Kierkegaard, Binswanger, May, and De Greeff, among others, did not subscribe to the primacy of the present. De Greeff, for example, according to Henri Ellenberger, says that only the one-year-old child lives in the present. The four-year-old has the concept of the day, the five-year-old the concept of yesterday and tomorrow, the eight-year-old the weeks, the 15-year-old the month, the 20-year-old the year, and the 40-year-old the years and decades. He adds that schizophrenics narrow their awareness of past and future, as do the mentally retarded and psychopaths.

However, Perls' views did form a tandem with an oversimplified image of Jean Paul Sartre's highly complex views on temporality. In *Nausea*, Sartre has his protagonist, Roquentin, paradoxically cast as a historian, wipe out all but present experience. Roquentin says:

> I looked anxiously around me: the present, nothing but the present. Furniture light and solid, rooted in its present, a table, a bed, a closet with a mirror—and me. The true nature of the present revealed itself: it was what exists, and all that was not present does not exist. The past did not exist. Not at all. Not in things, not even in my thoughts—Now I know: things are entire what they appear to be—and behind them . . . there is nothing.

This was a chilling resignation about the background factors in life, one with which Perls' slogans were compatible, lighting the way toward the obliteration of context. However, just as careful consideration of Perls will reveal concern with a fuller scope of human experience, so also will here-and-now limits be recognized as a burlesque of Sartre. In *Being and Nothingness* he says, for example:

> if we begin by isolating man on the instantaneous island of the present, . . . we have radically removed all methods of understanding his original relation to the past.

Following this sense of isolation, one may see that even in *Nausea*, where Roquentin sees nothing but the present, his state may be taken as a disease rather than as a commentary on the natural human condition. He feels imprisoned in the present and has become anxious upon realizing he no longer wants to allow time to stand still. He is deeply bothered that the needs for purpose, for formed relationship, for familiar activities and places are all uncertain of fulfillment. He says plaintively:

I have never before had such a strong feeling that I was devoid of secret dimensions, confined within the limits of my body, from which airy thoughts float up like bubbles. I build memories with my present self. I am cast out, forsaken in the present: *I vainly try to rejoin the past: I cannot escape.* (italics mine)

The agony of Roquentin's confinement to the present matches the stuckness with which all neurosis is identified. Perhaps Sartre saw Roquentin as tragically imprisoned by the present; perhaps, on the contrary, he saw him as regrettably unwilling to live in the present. Actually, there is nothing there, either to reside in or to escape from. Thinking of living *in the present* reminds one of the digital clock, an apt symbol for an isolated present. That this invention is more than a mundane convenience is illustrated by the observations of Tina Jacobowitz, a New Jersey educator, who noticed that children don't learn fractions as well as they used to. She recognized that the face-watch shows relationships no longer apparent in digitals. Concepts like before, after, whole, part, half-past and a quarter-to cannot be embodied by these timepieces. For all but an infinite fraction of a whole minute, time stands still, and always, whatever time the clock shows is the only time anybody can see. In the interests of simplicity, the digital expunges the context within which any specific time appears, thereby nullifying the visual experience of continuing transitional movement. The person who is oriented strictly to the present begets a comparable digital mentality. However, only by taking time's inevitable movement into account can one's attention be harmoniously directed to the full sweep of life's experience.

Nevertheless, as a psychological funnel for heightening attention, the here-and-now has served an important purpose. It helped to close the psychological distance between each person and life events. While trying to get into the *present*, one was incidentally impelled to get inside one's own *experience*. One found that what matters most is *what* is happening, with *whom* it is happening, *how* it is happening, *when* it is happening, how one *feels* about what is happening, and especially, what are the *consequences* of what is happening. The therapist will be more tuned in to fundamentals, though, in guiding a patient directly to that person's *function* and *awareness* rather than to "living in the present." Then the narrow band of experience created by high focus leads a person forward like an airplane homing in on the exact radio beam.

In order to coordinate the empowering intensity of the amplified experience with the more broadly encompassing reality in which everybody's experience is embedded, the therapist must be versatile enough to shuttle back and forth between different modes of engagement. Included within this comprehensiveness and adding a leavening sense of everyday humanity to therapy are some things ordinarily viewed as a waste of time, like exchanging recipes, joking around, reviewing a movie, or discussing vacation plans. The decor of someone's house, a description of a close friend, or reference to a stray adventure continues the expansion of simple interest of one person in another. Expanding the stories of the major events a person has experienced, seeing the implications of what she is doing, planning for new opportunities, feeling the importance of friendships — these and comparable human concerns all underscore the comprehensiveness of anyone's attention. This range of topic and style can help transform an otherwise dissociated experience into a self-evident part of a person's broader existence.

Shifting from one mode to another does not necessarily exclude high focus. Rather it sets the stage for it. Even the novel, condensed as it is, does not create a continual heart palpitation; nor must therapy. There is more to a representative human engagement than internal focus or beating pillows or penetrating confrontation or neuron-tripping shivers. So the risk of diluting the narrowed energy is often worth taking. Too little shifting — with only a highly concentrated emphasis on the "here and now" — will foreclose on much that matters: continuity of commitment, implications of one's acts, preparation for those complexities that require preparation, dependability, responsiveness to the demands that people will assuredly be exposed to, etc. When these inevitable requirements of living are chronically set aside for what should be only *temporary* technical purposes, alienation from large parts of the relevant society is one consequence; living life as a cliché is another.

A couple of examples of people infected by the stereotypes about present experience will help show some dissociative effects and some therapeutic invitations to escape from the present. Abigail, a 25-year-old woman, was alienated from her parents who objected for religious reasons to her living unmarried with a man. Though greatly distressed about her distance from them, Abigail stood firm on living with this man, whom she loved. She wanted urgently to reconcile with her parents, but not at the cost of her freedom of choice. In telling me her story, she spoke in the tone of a person younger than her 25 years, fighting her parents from a hopeless, childlike position. She knew much more than they did about contemporary living, but she spoke weakly anyway. I asked her to talk out loud to her parents, imagining them sitting in my office. She said they would ask her acidly whether she was going to get married. In response she said she didn't want to talk about it. Normally, in actual contact with them, she would either melt while dripping tears or go into a catatonic-like paralysis. I encouraged her to be as verbal as she could, cashing in on her knowledge by saying what she knew to be true. Then, taking both sides, she played out the following dialogue between her and her parents:

ABIGAIL: The reason we haven't gotten married is because we enjoy living together and I don't want to do something just because I'm supposed to. . . . I have to feel like it's important inside.
PARENTS: (Caustically) Well, isn't the church a good enough reason for you?
ABIGAIL: The church is very important to me. To me what is important is the spiritual part of it, to experience God. To me it's not just following the rules. According to our church, marriage is a sacrament. And I don't know why . . . I don't understand it at all. (Cries, looks confused again, resigned)

A crucial point was reached. For a moment Abigail did well at stating her position clearly. Then, characteristically, she got confused. She couldn't make the shift from firmly knowing something in her current environment to knowing it also with her parents. Her own truths, though she believed in them, were dissociated, therefore inapplicable when talking to her mother and father.

They were from an alien world. She told me, as she visualized them, that they were looking at her critically, neither understanding her nor even attempting to. What she felt—common for her—was that she was doing something wrong. In spite of her discomfort with her parents, she was still attached to her past. She needed them not only for the relationship itself, but also to overcome her feeling of being isolated from her entire past. Her sense of disconnection was like an amputation, cutting her away from her supports, leaving her with a cosmic whine. To feel bereft about losing her parents was sad enough, but the malaise was multiplied when she invalidated her lifetime of experience, which, of course, was not owned by them.

At this point I told her she looked as though she wanted to stop talking to them because she thought they wouldn't listen—but she might be stopping too soon. Whether they listened or not she needed to get the clarity that words provide. When I asked whether she would be willing to go on with the conversation, she returned to it. Again she played both parts, this time in a rather softer tone. Her parents told her how deeply hurt they were by her leaving the fold and said they were worried about her wasting her life, that she had no future. In response Abigail replied:

ABIGAIL: I don't think that's the way it is. I have a darn good future. To me what's important is what I have right now, not 20, 30, 50 years from now. And it should be. I don't know what's going on that long. What I have right now has nothing to do with the future. This is the way I have chosen to live my life now—it may change, I don't know (starting to get a marked whine in her voice again and beginning to sound contrived). What I know is that I am happy with today. (Unconvincing)

She seemed enmeshed in the liturgy about present experience. I explained to her that she had started out saying she had a darn good future, then abandoned this belief by discounting the future entirely. I explained that she probably does have expectations about the future, some subtle and some quite evident. I suggested that her parents thought she was wrong when she told them the future doesn't count—rather than, as she had started to say, that she had a different opinion about her future. She probably thought she was wrong, too, because the future did count, even though this was contradicted by the people she associated with, who were heavily present-oriented. Her confusion left her without a leg to stand on. At this point, I suggested she speak to her parents again, saying what was actually true for her.

ABIGAIL: When you say I have no future, that has no merit, that if I'm not married it could end too easily and if I were married it couldn't and wouldn't. Nobody could just drop out of it. . . . I don't think this is true. . . . I believe we have a very strong commitment to each other. . . . Whatever problems come up between us, we think in terms of long-term, not in terms of it's good for now only and we'll not be married because it's easier to pick up and leave.

By this time, her voice had lost all trace of whine. She was clear in her gaze, whereas ordinarily she had a questioning look on her face. She now seemed unconcerned about whether her parents accepted what she was saying. She obviously believed what she said; when I asked her how it felt to say it, she simply replied, "Clear." She now looked well grounded and later remarked about her lifetime of accumulated understandings, "It's a process of changing what I was taught and taking everything else I've learned and putting it all together."

What was apparent in Abigail's mind-set was the ascendant place of the present. This focus permitted her to have a relationship that her background would not allow. Since she could not manage the contradiction, she had to cut out her parents' influence, unnecessarily detaching also from other large regions of her life. She had mistakenly equated her parents' influence with her past life. But her past—anybody's past—was much larger than her parents' attitudes and could remain as hospitable background to her current life whether her parents accepted her or not. This whole interwoven mosaic of her past, present, and future had become hopelessly confused, much as in the brainwashed person returning from Chinese internment to American culture. Putting it all together was not as hopeless a prospect as she assumed, once she recognized the truth in her own argument. Once she believed in her actual future instead of relying on dissociated jargon, her rights to her relationship to the man she loved were seen as a part of the simple continuity of her life.

Another patient, Ann, a 35-year-old recent social work graduate, described her imprisonment in the present differently when she said:

> I used to be very goal oriented. . . . Once my marriage broke up, I lost my sense of future, I lost my dreams and I lost feeling that I could get them. When I was younger I thought I could always get whatever I wanted—which may be part of being young. I generally . . . got what I wanted. Now I don't have that sense—once in a while I do get that sense—the sense that I can get what I want. But I don't really feel it the way I used to feel it. And I also don't have dreams—real dreams. I don't imagine myself married—I can't even imagine what that's like anymore—or even having a child—I can't imagine.
>
> I came across something I have written—it's about losing dreams and needing to create new ones and if you don't, you fall into an abyss—I realized cognitively years ago that I needed to create new things that I wanted but underneath there isn't anything—or there's a feeling that I can't get them.

Ann's words have a familiar ring, reminiscent of Sartre's Roquentin and also common among depressed people, who characteristically experience no future—only loss. Their attention is restricted to a dim present while paradoxically shunning those parts of the present which might enliven them. Ann, however, was not typical. Though speaking the words of depression, she was also energetic. She spoke rapidly, almost catapulting herself into nextness, but every time she got there her experience was not new. Her sequences of moment-to-moment experience crowded each other into a conglomerate present, like the pianist whose individual notes have no distinctiveness.

It became apparent to me that Ann's loss of her sense of future caused her to require too little from her experiences. Requirements propel people forward toward the consequences of any experience. It was necessary for Ann to begin to have requirements of me, her friends, her job, her patients, herself. She got the message and translated it into seeking new work benefits. Instead of remaining fixed in the part-time, temporary job she had, with which she had previously been willing to stay for as long as it lasted, she found a new job, one which would have a greater bearing on her future.

This took some doing. She had to move to a remote community, one not normally attractive to her and from which she intended to move later on. This job and community provided opportunities for a higher level of experience, with increased professional respect, licensing hours, colleagues more compatible with her, release from the big city rat race, and a clear base for getting another job later in a city where she wanted to live. She took this job with a measured eye for what would be best for her in the long run. However, even the short run was rewarding. Her visage was brighter, her language clearer, her clothes more self-respectful, and her anxiety practically gone. She was not even afraid of me anymore. But she couldn't live in this town forever; it was just not her city. When she complained about this, it became apparent that her restrictive sense of the present died hard; her myopic habits still led her to say that she didn't know what she was doing there. She knew very well what she was doing there—getting exactly what she planned to get. Actually, when she let go of her stereotypes about sterile towns, she found she was having the time of her life in this very town; she was active more fruitfully than ever right in the center of a new community, where what she did had personal impact and caused change. She also found excellent companionship. But what she had not found was a man to live with or marry, which she missed greatly. Nevertheless, although the future never reveals itself in visible line, it is clearly out there and she knows she is inexorably headed through it.*

The severance of continuity by people with a here-and-now orientation is further illustrated by David Hellerstein, who has

*Recently, a year after writing this, I received an announcement of her wedding.

written about men who do not want to "grow up," the so-called Peter Pan people. The men he describes are charming, intelligent, and temporarily successful. On the face of it, they live beautifully; they make easy relationships, play happily, do their work well. But none of them can allow himself the dividends from these accomplishments. They just cop out when other people in the same position would make their moves, either into advances in their work or into fulfilling relationships. These are people who milk the present of all it offers — excitement, novelty, romance, adoration. When they feel crowded — either by new requirements or, contrarily, by a sense of repetition — instead of freshening up their experiences by attention to whatever might naturally be next, they must start all over again — another place, another person, another job.

After each of these episodic moves, these people catch on agreeably before they are faced again with the barriers of boredom, complexity, commitment, or a newly unpleasant task. These barriers do, of course, arrive anyway for all of them, but for a while they are able dissociatively to maintain the illusion that all that matters is what is happening now. As Hellerstein says about one of these men, "He may seem seriously committed to a job or a relationship, but he's ready to flip over to another existence at any moment. When real commitments have to be made, he'll sneak away in a second; he won't settle down. He lives in defiance of biological clocks and parental expectations and glories in the illusion of endless youth." The present is often beautiful for these people, addictively compelling, and it must be repeated over and over, narrowing their worlds into futureless novelty.

A polar opposite to the jolly neurosis of Peter Pan is the grim fate of Meursault in Camus' *The Stranger*. In this classic novel, Camus portrayed with insight both revelatory and prophetic the sameness which accrues to the rootless, meaningless life. Meursault, through a series of fortuitous events over which he seemed to have no control, wound up killing a man. He had no personal stake in killing him, yet there he was doing it. Nor did it make any difference, since everything was simply *as it was*. What he did during his murder trial had little to do with his obvious stake in the trial. He observed events quite simply and only occasionally did consequence or meaning seep through. Even though his life was on the line, he would lose interest quickly. He observed, "The only things that really caught my attention were occasional phrases . . . gestures, and some elaborate tirades—but these were isolated patches." Everything he experienced begot much the same nihilistic tone as everything else, though the events themselves were highly diverse. Meursault reported to the reader his pathetic loss of continuity by saying, "When, one morning, the jailer informed me I'd now been six months in jail, I believed him—but the words conveyed nothing to my mind. To me it seemed like one and the same day that had been going on since I'd been in my cell, and that I'd been doing the same thing all the time."

Aside from the natural sameness which anyone might experience in a jail cell, the sameness for Meursault was only an exaggeration of the previously familiar sameness in his life. What he did the day after his mother died had little to do with the fact she had died. For him, as for the Peter Pan people, the nows of life were simply endless repetitions, a disease from which Meursault never recovered. As a report of one man's experience—in a novel at that—this tragedy could be easily dismissed. As a classic novel, though, touching the sensibilities of generations of insightful people, it rings the bells of recognition that qualify it as notable social commentary.

From these accounts of the stuckness of present-oriented people—my patients, the Peter Pan people and Camus' Meursault—it is apparent that living in the narrow present can be crippling. It is no substitute for experiencing the drama of life in all of its complex dimensions. While the here-and-now has provided people with insight into the power engendered by narrowed attention, it is important to add humanistic weight in the struggle to allot technology no more than its proportional credit in the expansion of human experience. The emphasis on technique dramatically upstaged what was always methodologically crucial in gestalt therapy, the common human engagement. This includes much that is ordinary: support, curiosity, kindness, bold language, laughter, cynicism, assimilation of tragedy, rage, gentleness, and toughness. This common consciousness, always active but given less popular recognition, is necessary for going beyond revelatory technology. Simple humanity can, indeed, generate fascination and in concert with supporting technology highlight the drama, therefore the reality, of each lived life. These broader interests, especially as they are expressed by the novelist, may help therapists to encompass all they can about how people live, not only *here* but also *there*, not only *now* but also *then*. It is too late for the fictional Meursault and uninteresting to many of his nihilistic counterparts in real life, but it is nevertheless worth noticing that there is a future to which we *may* look ahead. But whether we look or not, it will come, it will come!

References

Atwood, Margaret, *Lady Oracle*. New York: Avon, 1977.

Atwood, Margaret, *Surfacing*, New York: Popular Library, 1972.

Anderson, Maxwell. As quoted in Logan, Joshua, *Josh: My Up and Down, In and Out Life*. New York: Dell Books, 1976.

Barr, Amelia E., *Jan Verder's Wife*. New York: Dodd, Mead & Co., 1985.

Berkvist, Robert, *New York Times*, April 10, 1977.

Borges, Jorge Luis, *A Personal Anthology*, New York: Grove Press, Inc., 1967.

Bruner, Jerome, *Myth and Identity in Myth and Mythmaking*, edited by Henry A. Murray. New York: George Braziller, 1960.

Camus, Albert, *The Stranger*, New York: Knopf, 1942.

Canby, Vincent, *New York Times*, March 13, 1983.

Carroll, Lewis. *Alice's Adventures in Wonderland and Through the Looking Glass*. New York: New American Library, 1973.

Chase, Mildred Portnoy, *Just Being at the Piano*, Culver City, CA: Peace Press, 1974.

Davies, Robertson, *Fifth Business*, New York: Penguin, 1970.

De Greeff. As quoted by Ellenberger, Henri in *Existence*, edited by May, Angel, and Ellenberger. New York: Basic Books, 1958.

Doctorow, E. L. *Loon Lake*. New York: Random House, 1980.

Doctorow, E. L. "The Passion of Our Calling," in *The New York Times Book Review*. August 25, 1985.

Dreiser, Theodore, *Sister Carrie*, New York: Harper, 1900.

Eiseley, Loren, *All the Strange Hours*, New York: Scribner's, 1975.

Erasmus, *The Praise of Folly*, Ann Arbor Paperback, 1958.

Erickson, M. H. and Rossi, E. L., *Hypnotherapy*, New York: Irvington, 1979.

Forster, E. M., *The Writer's Craft*, edited by John Hersey, New York: Random House, 1973.

Fowles, John, *Daniel Martin*, New York: Signet, 1977.

Gardner, John, *On Becoming a Novelist*, New York: Harper & Row, 1983.

Godwin, Gail, *A Mother and Two Daughters*, New York: Viking, 1982.

Gombrich, E. H., *The Story of Art*, New York: Phaidon, 1950.

Haley, Jay, *Uncommon Therapy*, New York: Norton, 1973.

Hellerstein, David. "The Peter Pan Principle." In *Esquire*, October 1983.

Howard, Maureen, *New York Times Book Review*, April 25, 1982.

Irving, John, *The World According to Garp*, New York: E. P. Dutton, 1978.

Jacobi, Derek. Interview with Michiku Kakutani in *The International Herald Tribune*. February 11, 1985.

Jacobowitz, Tina, letter to the editor, *New York Times* magazine section, January 23, 1983.

James, Henry, *Notes to Novelists*, London: J. M. Dent & Sons Ltd., 1914.

Johnson, Diane. Review of *Austin and Mabel* by Polly Longworth, New York Times Book Review, March 4, 1985.

Johnson, Spencer. *The Precious Present*. New York: Doubleday, 1984.

Kafka, Franz. *The Castle*. New York: Knopf, 1954.

Kosinski, Jerzy. Interview in *Psychology Today* by Sheehy, Gail, December 1977.

Krishna, Gopi, *Kundalini*, Boulder, CO: Shambala, 1967.

Kundera, Milan, *The Unbearable Lightness of Being*, New York: Harper & Row, 1984.

Lifton, Robert Jay, *Thought Reform and the Psychology of Totalism*, New York: Norton, 1963.

Masson, Jeffrey M. *The Assault on Truth: Freud's Suppression of the Seduction Theory*, New York: Farrar, Strauss & Giroux, Inc., 1984.

Melville, Herman. *Moby Dick*, edited by Hayford, H., and Parker, H. New York: Norton, 1967.

Miller, James E. Jr., ed. *Theory of Fiction, Henry James*, Lincoln, Neb.: University of Nebraska Press, 1972.

Moore, Marion R., "Principles of Ericksonian Induction of Hypnosis," in *Ericksonian Approaches to Hypnosis and Psychotherapy*, ed. J. Zeig, New York: Brunner/Mazel, 1982.

Nin, Anais, *The Novel of the Future*. Athens, OH: Ohio University Press, 1985. Distributed by Harper & Row, New York.

O'Neill, Eugene, *The Hairy Ape and Other Plays*, London: Cape, 1923.

Perls, F. S., *Ego, Hunger and Aggression*, London: George Allen and Unwin, 1947.

Perls, F. S., "Four Lectures" in *Gestalt Therapy Now*, edited by Joen Fagan and Irma Shepard. Palo Alto: Science and Behavior Books, 1970.

Perls, F. S., Hefferline, R. and Goodman, P. *Gestalt Therapy*. New York: Julian Press, 1951.

Plimpton, George, ed. *Writers at Work, Paris Review Interviews*, New York: Viking Press, 1976.

Polster, Erving and Miriam Polster, *Gestalt Therapy Integrated*, New York: Brunner/Mazel, 1973; Vintage Books, 1974.

Proust, Marcel, *Remembrance of Things Past*, New York: Random House, 1924.

Pym, Barbara, *Excellent Women*, New York: Harper & Row, 1952.

Richardson, Ralph. Interview with Nightingale, Benedict, *The New York Times*, December 9, 1982.

Rosen, Sidney. *My Voice Will Go With You*. New York: Norton, 1982.

Salinger, J. D. *Catcher in the Rye*. Boston: Little, Brown, 1951.

Sargent, William, *Battle for the Mind*, London: Heinemann, 1957.

Sartre, Jean Paul, *Being and Nothingness*, New York: Philosophical Library, 1956.

Sartre, *Nausea*, New York: New Directions, 1964.

Saville, Jonathan, "Ineffable Weirdness" in *The Reader*. San Diego, CA., April 21, 1983.

Schwartz, Lynne Sharon, *Disturbances in the Field*, New York: Harper & Row, 1983.

Shah, Idries, *Tale of the Dervishes*, New York: Dutton, 1970.

Shawn, Wallace and Andre Gregory, *My Dinner with Andre*, New York: Grove Press, 1981.

Simenon, Georges. *The Cat*. New York: Harcourt Brace Jovanovich, 1976.

Strasberg, Lee, Mike Nichols interview with Barbara Gelb, *The New York Times Magazine*. May 27, 1984.

Stevenson, Robert Lewis. *Dr. Jekyll and Mr. Hyde*. New York: Bantam, 1981.

Styron, William, *Sophie's Choice*, New York: Random House, 1980.

Terkel, Studs, *Working*, New York: Pantheon, 1972.

Updike, John, *The Centaur*, New York: Knopf, 1963.

Walker, R. L., *China Under Communism*, London: Allen & Unwin, 1956.

Welty, Eudora. *One Writer's Beginnings*. New York: Warner Books, 1985, p. 16.

Index